ARTHUR KELETI

The Imperfect Secret

ARTHUR KELETI

The Imperfect Secret

with the help of
Zsuzsanna Szvetelszky, social psychologist
including the novella "A Bad Day,"
by award-winning sci-fi writer
Mihály Toochee Kovács

ISBN-10: 153759172X
ISBN-13: 978-1537591728
Printed and bound in the United States of America

Trademarked names may appear in this book.
Rather than use a trademark symbol with every occurrence of a trademarked name,
we use the names only in an editorial fashion and to the benefit of the trademark owner,
with no intention of infringement of the trademark.

Senior Project Manager: Viktor Justin
(http://www.viktorjustin.com)
Translation: EDMF & James Davidson
Senior Editor: James Davidson
Copy Editor: Ferenc Mező
Compositor & Cover post production work: Tamás Csapó
(https://www.behance.net/csapotamas)
Cover Design Idea: Arthur Keleti & Viktor Justin
Cover Design: Tae Boriboonhiranthana
(https://www.behance.net/taeboribunhiranthana)

Distributed to the book trade worldwide by
http://www.arthurkeleti.com, e-mail: orders@arthurkeleti.com
For information on translations, please contact
http://www.arthurkeleti.com directly at info@arthurkeleti.com
Arthur Keleti's books may be purchased in bulk for academic, corporate,
or promotional use. eBook versions and licenses are also available for most titles.
For more information, reference our Special Bulk Sales–eBook Licensing web page
at http://www.arthurkeleti.com/info/bulksales.

The information in this book is distributed on an "as is" basis, without warranty.
Although every precaution has been taken in the preparation of this work, the author
shall not have any liability to any person or entity with respect to any loss or damage caused
or alleged to be caused directly or indirectly by the information contained in this work.

CHAPTERS

ACKNOWLEDGMENTS

To my parents, for helping me find my way in walking, thinking, and in life itself. Without them I would understand much less about the world and myself.

To my friend András, who understands what I'm thinking almost before I do.

To my friend Dimi, who always shows me that "everything is different."

To my friend Zóra, who still speaks nicely to me even when all my patience has been exhausted.

สำหรับน้องเต้ คนที่ทำให้ผมเข้าใจว่าโลกใบนี้สงบสุขและสวยงาม

To my proofreader and friend Zsuzsa Szvetelszky, with whom I have been able to roam a world I didn't even know existed. She has inspired me more than she knows.

To my friend and colleague Viktor Justin, who forges and smooths the path in front of me with his tireless energy and inexhaustible enthusiasm.

To my friend, the sci-fi writer Mihály Toochee Kovács, thick as thieves as we are together in Orwell's future.

To Balázs Kovács, who helped me understand all that was in our minds on the model of assessing secrets.

To T-Systems and all my colleagues, who have tolerated my eccentricity over the last 10 years working together.

To colleagues and friends at the Voluntary Cyber Defence Collaboration (KIBEV), who always open up new perspectives for me with their wisdom and insights.

To all cybersecurity professionals, who are currently fighting on the front line of information technology. I've learned a lot from you, take care! Come home safely!

To Alphaville for their fantastic song "Victory of Love," which got me started on all the difficult days.

And first and foremost to you, dear Kiwi. While you're no longer around to see this, I know you wouldn't have been interested anyway :)

PROLOGUE

*"I can't tell this to anyone,
so I'm telling everyone..."*

While working on his incandescent lamp, Thomas Edison said that he discovered thousands of ways not to make an incandescent lamp. As the idea of this book was taking shape in my mind, after some twenty years of cybersecurity struggles, I began to feel just like the renowned inventor did. I could mention countless ways not to create security. During these years I have discovered exactly what I do not know. But I never thought that my journey into the realm of secrets, and my immersion into the social research aspect of the topic, would yield discoveries more trying and challenging for my faith in cybersecurity than anything before. I came to realize that the wild bull of the digital world has broken loose, tossing societies, states, companies and families this way and that, as they try to hold onto its broad back; so completely out of control that not even we, security experts, can guarantee their safety.

Today global companies wrangle with secret service agencies or steal data from one another, while states hack each other's political parties. We come up with increasingly undecipherable encryptions, as self-appointed hackers and the cyber soldiers of terrorist states go around arbitrating on the roads of cyberspace, and our children, parents or spouses are blackmailed by cyber criminals. The problems posed by cybersecurity have outgrown those caused by drugs. All this is happening with incredible speed and with immeasurable amounts of data, which will give way to the autocracy of machines to an unprecedented extent.

Amid this huge cloud of dust I too am holding onto the bull's back along with the others, and while swallowing the dust and struggling to stay in the saddle, the lovely voice of a reporter asks me, "So Mr. Keleti, what can we do now?" I simply adjust the sleeve of my jacket with one firm move and calmly say, "Change your bad passwords and be extremely careful with your personal data! Thank you!"

Well, not really. Actually, truth be told, given what is currently happening to our digital property out there in cyberspace, a good password helps us to stay on the back of that bull about as much as a good cowboy hat would. Because the problem goes far beyond cyberspace and information technology: Yes, passwords and mobile phones have been precisely engineered, but it is general human priorities that are at work when it comes to what we store in them, and both security experts and hackers can only be onlookers in the process. Together with my friend, the social psychologist Zsuzsa Szvetelszky, we tried to put our fingers on what the problem could be. We talked for ages, you can't even begin to imagine how long. And then we figured it out.

We found the reason, and let there be no mistake, it did not reassure me at all. It won't reassure you either. But perhaps, if I dare say out loud what I have understood as to why an entire industry has viewed cybersecurity from a completely wrong angle, I can inspire others to rethink their views on the issue of privacy versus security, which has been the focus of so many social, professional and legal debates in the past few years. This new perspective may inspire corporate decision-makers to seek new ways to protect their data, fellow experts to consider the option of developing brand new and radically different applications, and families to look beyond their cyber fences.

I'm warning you now that this book contains no new cybersecurity algorithms, zero day vulnerabilities or new sociology models. It contains all that I have discovered about cybersecurity and its implications for mankind, along with realizations, trains of thought and issues relating to our near future. This is what you get if you choose to sit with me on the back of the bull, and bow your head to Edison's spirit: We'll figure out together if we can find a new way to stay in the saddle. What I also offer to anybody who can cope with this journey is an invitation, courtesy of my friend, the award-winning sci-fi writer Mihály 'Toochee' Kovács, to a day in the life of an average New York family in the near future, rather alarming from a cybersecurity point of view, in his novella "A Bad Day."

CHAPTER 1

INTRODUCTION

Silence is golden,
watching is silver,
gate-keeping is bronze

Back in the old days it was enough to know that silence is golden. Today we also have to learn how to protect our secrets, which requires a new technical skill. What is secret today was not necessarily secret before, and what used to be secret is no longer today. It follows that different things need to be kept secret in different ways than before. More specifically, it's not the data or the information that needs encryption, but the true secrets. Everyone has secrets, and someone else will always be interested in that secret, otherwise it wouldn't be one. What kinds of data or information can be kept secret for somebody and how? And what is a secret in cyberspace anyway? That's what this book is about.

A secret is never an independent phenomenon, but always one of connection and network. The most crucial and widely quoted statement from the 2013 Gartner Report predicts that the time when we will no longer be able to protect 75% of our data using available technology is as close as 2020. Technical experts, however, seem in general to ignore the human aspects of secrets, the human factor, despite the fact that we are surrounded by more and more secrets, and their quantity and complexity is growing in proportion to the increasing complexity and scale of society.

In the past there was much less information around, and it was possible to become a polymath, knowing far more about the world than the majority of people; today this is unrealistic. There are no longer omniscient people, only those who know a part of the information. At the same time, increasing amounts of data and information are being created and the significance of particular data for particular parties now depends on a number of factors.

Even if we avoid doing anything that could be frowned upon, there is still reason for anxiety: tens of thousands of laws apply to every citizen, as well as countless rules and norms of social practice, we are bound to violate one or another of them from time to time. You start wondering, good gracious, what could I have done on Christmas afternoon to offend poor Aunt Bertha? Anything really, without knowing it. I can make a mistake at any time. This is why a lot of people are concerned about the implications of being watched. I mean, what if I make a mistake?

Every one of us behaves now and then in a way that is reproachable. Something that tarnishes a reputation can come out about anyone. This results in an existential kind of fear. When you are alone, you feel more at ease scratching you head or eating a steak with your hands. I, for one, love eating directly from the fridge, standing in front of it with the door open. I'm telling you, yesterday's pizza tastes better in the cold electric light of the fridge than at the table, but I'm not so keen on sharing this little habit of mine with just anyone... although perhaps that horse has already bolted.

You may also be worried about doing something forbidden without realizing. This can be an unconscious fear, as you do not know exactly what is forbidden and what is really secret. The uncertain boundary between these two is a basic cause of confusion these days. Prompted by his interview with ex-NSA employee Edward Snowden, who leaked classified information from the US secret service, reporter and talk-show host John Oliver asked people in the street if they were concerned by the fact that the secret service agency listens to their conversations. They said no, but when asked if they were aware that the secret service agency could see shots of them naked, their "dick pics" to be precise, they were appalled. We are concerned if people find out something about us that may be more or less intimate, but it's still our privacy: we are worried that we either violate some rule or that our reputation could be damaged. We don't want our neighbors to know that we brush our teeth inside out.

In privacy you do not do forbidden things, you just relax. You do things you would not do in public. For example, you wear a stretched T-shirt or allow yourself a loud burp. You might visit websites as well as view and store documents that you would not want others to know about. This latter phenomena has grown so widespread that one of the characters in Suicide Squad, a movie premiered in the summer of 2016, tells his buddies that if he dies, he wants them to kill his murderer and clear his browsing history.

In archaic communities, everyone – 99 percent of society – could smell what their neighbor was cooking, and see their underpants drying in the garden: there was transparency in everyday life that most people have become unaccustomed to in the modern age and in big cities. Since people used to live very similar lives, they rarely thought about living in any other way. Every minute of their lives was regulated by some norm or rule relating to the weather or farming, to religion or folk traditions. The only things that could interfere with this were unpredictable occurrences from the outside, like a hail storm, wolves or an attack from another horde. If you stuck to the rules, you had a good chance of getting food, either from your own farming or from the common goods.

This way of life has undergone dramatic changes in the past century or two. These days, stepping out sleepily onto the balcony and sipping coffee in your PJs, we aren't overly delighted to hear the familiar voice of a neighbor from the balcony next door saying, "Morning, Andy! Same good coffee as yesterday? Where are you hiding that lovely girlfriend of yours? By the way, I have your mail." Of course, letters have previously been snatched from royal couriers too, but back then not very many people sent letters other than monarchs...

Today's era of exchanging secrets was preceded in Eastern Europe and the Soviet Union, for example, by a period that shaped the idea of privacy for the people who lived there in a rather unique way. The one-sided and systematic monitoring that came into place after 1945 was an existential threat. You could easily get into trouble if you were found to have said or done something that was not to the liking of the contemporary political regime. This is fundamentally different from what we are talking about today, since the monitoring of the Soviet Union took place as part of a hierarchy, i.e. the complex system of those monitoring and those monitored was controlled vertically, from the top to the bottom. This vertical structure did not allow any feedback or reciprocity; fear, vulnerability and insecurity were present at all levels. The age-old saying of "loose lips sink ships" strengthened to the point that many people believed passivity to be the only possible survival strategy. Look at today's China, for example, where we still see similar reactions.

However, people today are under more observation than ever before, and not as part of any top-down political system, but rather in a horizontal relation: people follow and "stalk" one another using various social apps. They even record each other's offline communications: in the past, when two people were mowing a meadow with their scythes, neither could possibly record anything with a device hidden in their clothes. Dictaphones still have an LED light indicating that recording is taking place. What is more, there used to be a beeping sound during a telephone conversation to let you know that the other party was calling you from a phone box. Thus there were several ways people could tell that their conversation was being recorded. But alas, the recording LED of dictaphones seems to be fading. If you are looking for a program to record telephone conversations today, you are likely to find a warning in the description that it is up to you to tell your conversation partner that you are recording the conversation, as your partner will no longer have any way of knowing. It is considered appropriate to inform the other party about the recording, because otherwise they have lost control completely. Not only will they not realize that their words are being recorded, but they will also have no idea what the person recording their words, their sighs, their booming or raised voice, intends to do with the recording. Meeting members of the media now and then it has sometimes occurred to me that the warning sign "On air" in television and radio studios has become somewhat of a paradox since we can listen to the sound of baby monitors even from far away on our smart phones. "Fine, so is there anywhere left that is not On air?"

As the famous US writer John Steinbeck put it: "No one wants advice, only corroboration." People who, by virtue of their mandate, position or access to certain devices, can make decisions about what to say on various issues, what is secret and what is not, used to be called gatekeepers. These days, the question is rather whether any intelligence or function exists or can be created that can decide, instead of a person, whether something is a secret or not. Today this function is reserved for humans only, it has not been automated yet: there is no software to identify secrets, there are only owners of secrets, but the model itself is far from unrealistic. Looking at this the other way around, today even private persons can be gatekeepers. They have their hands full as they pass on, post or share the information at their disposal. The operator of the channel can, of course, decide whether or not to remove the information (to delete a comment or an article for instance). So from a certain point of view, such limiting functions do exist, but it is essentially the individual who decides (particularly when it comes to timing). In government or corporate communication this gatekeeper function may be somewhat different, typically it would be communication through organizational explanations, a kind of interpreting filter. For instance, when the US administration decides how to explain or interpret a cybersecurity case, they have to decide whether it should be considered a criminal case or an attack on the country. There can be a number of scenarios: A Chinese or Russian hacker attack, a terrorist event or a North-Korean incident.

A number of technological attempts have been made to categorize and sort the information stored in phones and computers (e.g. by separating private and business use in mobile phones by software) but, to be honest, not even this can be achieved without a hitch, and we haven't yet mentioned real secrets and particularly sensitive information. In such cases, many security experts play their joker "encryption" card, i.e. let's encrypt everything we can in a given environment, which in principle trumps everything. But in actual fact, if we encrypt everything that's important to us, we can easily end up in a situation where everything becomes secret, but then nothing really is. In other words, once we have opened the encrypted box, then it may remain open. If an operating system or telephone is attacked by data-stealing malware while it is in use, then the encryption is not worth much, since at the time of the theft we were working with the decoded data. Technology experts have yet to come up with something smart enough to tackle this problem.

The situation is made even more difficult because no one really knows what and to whom they can hand over, forward, show or tell. I wish I had a dollar for every time I have been asked "Can I send this?" to which the best answer most of the time was, "It depends..." So we are guessing, trying to follow rules of varying quality and depth, and trying to learn from our mistakes.

CHAPTER 2

A CYBER STORM IS BREWING

*The taboo, the gossip, the public,
and the hacker – a one-act tragedy
about the informal turn*

Information is a volatile power, that we only possess until somebody else learns about it. What is more, it represents power only if we know its content as well, unlike other powers such as money. In the 21st century, however, money has also become information. Just think that today the vast majority of our economic systems operate in such a way that they are fed with information, without which we would have no working systems whatsoever. Stock exchange trading is a good example of this. Over the last couple of years we have learned that money itself can also be completely digital; Bitcoin, a digital currency, even has exchange rates, it is traded, and both individuals and companies keep part of their assets in this currency.

I have figured out why IT systems and tools require increasing amounts of resources during their development, and why they become increasingly complex. It is because people create them, and we are simply like this. If something is better, it is more. If something is more, it is more expensive. If something is bigger, it is more complex. That is why the systems we create follow this model during their development, becoming ever more hungry for information while also producing increasing amounts of data. If there is more information, appearing at a faster rate, then there is obviously a serious risk in terms of who receives such information from where and when. Unfortunately, the increasingly frequent terrorist attacks in Europe are a compelling example. In this respect almost every second question in the media and in everyday conversations is why secret service agencies and the police did not know of them earlier. They had access to a mass of data about where and when these terrorists arrived in the European Union, when they communicated and with whom by their mobile phones or via their email accounts. So why could law enforcement agencies not draw the appropriate conclusions from this data to prevent the catastrophe?

The answer is very simple, unfortunately: the amount of available data is so huge that it is simply impossible to analyze it. By 2020, 44 zettabytes of data will be circulated every year on the internet alone – a figure which does not even include the enormous systems of corporations and governments. This number is equal to hundreds of millions of HD films. Incidentally, this will be generated by 27 billion devices connected to the network. If there is more information, appearing at a faster rate, then another serious risk is not knowing who might receive such information, from where and when. The simple reason for this is that the amount of available information is so great that although we can access it, read it freely and analyze it, it is increasingly difficult to decide what is important and what is not; understanding the network of connections to which the data belongs is an even more difficult and trying task.

Not only the amount but also the quality of information has changed. Some 10 or 20 years ago people could simply lie about something: "Of course we are on good terms, of course everything is alright," or they could keep themselves aloof: "Uh, I don't want to talk about that right now," and there would have been a much smaller chance of their being caught or their secret found out and revealed. This has brought about changes in both everyday and electronic communication. Instead of a simple lie or denial we commonly hear for example that "my relationship is complicated." People have found new and interesting ways to avoid lying in a specific, fascinating, and mystical form.

The following invitation heard at weddings always makes me smile: "If anyone objects to this marriage, let them speak now or forever hold their peace." The tense silence particularly in the first few seconds after this is thrilling. Everybody is wondering whether anybody will spill the beans in front of hundreds of people at the church, the truth that nobody talks about but several people may know. Will anybody speak? As an interesting business and social experiment, I have already tried this method several times during project negotiations or at the end of meetings. I can recommend it to everyone, it is quite educational. It is none other than a taboo.

In her dissertation, Hungarian sociologist Andrea Rajkó examines this mostly hidden social phenomenon of our modern age. The topic of secrecy is related extremely closely to the topic of taboos. Just as secrets have a different role in today's societies compared to centuries ago, taboos are also changing. Taboos are not just hidden manifestations, they are contradictory as well: they are problematic to observe and describe, but constitute an integral part of social standards. Taboos were known in society in the clear and unwritten laws of ancient groups, which were much more transparent than the regulatory frameworks of modern societies. Today it is much more difficult to find taboos in the "classic sense" of the word. Is it a taboo to tattoo your ex-lovers' names on your back? Not so much anymore.

Yet taboos are no longer just silent traditions. At the beginning of the 21st century, the questions as to what becomes a taboo have multiplied in the light of global society, different emerging opinions, and infocommunications technology. Self-organizing information flows between not just individuals but also groups, create new processes to expose secrets, or to tolerate the departure from social norms. Those who share a list of romantic trysts tattooed on their back on Instagram may even be cool.

Many see the number and role of taboos declining, pointing towards the impact of the Internet to explain their argument. By contrast, Andrea Rajkó argues that the Internet plays a key role in turning many social phenomena into taboos, as the World Wide Web means we can monitor and learn others' opinions more thoroughly and in more detail than ever before. What is significant is not only the vast quantity of opinions that we can read online, but also the great variety of categories they fall into: this variety makes it difficult to determine what is a taboo and what is not. There is no point in thinking that our modern society must be more accommodating than earlier eras: curiously, the development of technology can even help to propagate the number of taboos and strengthen their impact. We no longer know which people deem what to be a taboo, nor, if something is a taboo, then how many people subscribe to this view and where.

While the number of mysteries, taboos and secrets are increasing on account of the development of information systems, these systems themselves are also becoming increasingly complicated. Moreover, information by itself is also becoming increasingly complex. So there is a huge amount of information (think of the 44 zettabytes of data expected by 2020), in which it is increasingly difficult to search, and which by itself is becoming more complex, difficult, and packed with secrets and taboos. It is an ideal place to look for errors to exploit.

The quality of the attacks that take advantage of errors are improved and refined at the same rate as this complexity grows. These trends must be followed because the security level of the services provided in the cyber world, together with their quality of protection and the security system itself, are changing so fast, that we are forced to keep moving constantly. Similarly, law enforcement bodies in the physical world must keep improving on a continuous basis, as the criminal elements keep pace with their innovations and adapt. You have probably seen a donkey moving forward towards a carrot on a stick dangled in front of it, despite the fact that it will obviously never reach it. That is exactly what this is about. I leave it to your imagination whether the security system is the carrot or the donkey.

That is why security experts emphasize that as soon as a user, a company or the state enters cyberspace, it finds itself in a constant cycle, which is characterized by updating anti-virus applications and continuously fighting against extortion attempts on the users' side, whereas companies and state players dig a bottomless pit of seemingly infinite human and material resources. This way, every technological innovation makes the task of security experts exceedingly difficult. Unless machines can take this off our shoulders, it will remain an endless human struggle.

What is causing this cycle? This is where the motives and role of hackers fit in in the really complex matter of stealing data or attacking IT systems. Hackers come from the youngest generation of society, and many "stick to their last" even after they mature. The meaning of the word 'hacker' has changed significantly since the 1980s and '90s, but the phrase must have been sounded like a fine appetizer in France even back then. In the early 21st century it means a person with a special way of thinking, who likes to look behind things, take them apart, understand how they work and make them better or more effective.

Good hackers differ from bad hackers in the latter point (white hats vs black hats, ethical hackers vs malicious hackers). Young people with a hacker's nature are susceptible to new things, they learn and adapt quickly and absorb technology virtually on their mother's knee; just think about little children with tablets. It is no coincidence that the secret service, military, public administration, and law enforcement agencies of every developed and emerging country today try to acquire these young people for themselves in time.

Yet this is exactly what the leaders of terrorist organizations and dictatorial regimes aim for too. And if none of them succeed, these youths can still become hacktivists – e.g. Anonymous members – or unreliable employees, who will probably leak or sell confidential information on the black market of the Internet, on the dark web, eventually. Information technology forged its path in both warfare and secret service activities, thereby triggering changes that require a labor force that is already familiar with the virtual world. In fact we are witnessing a new cold war arms race, in which cyber war weapons are developed and soldiers are recruited. This war takes place on IT battlefields, and soldiers sitting in front of their computers are waging battle against each other. Therefore, contrary to all appearances, countries, terrorists or companies do not necessarily want to catch young hackers to prevent their fall from grace, but rather to prevent them from causing such damage to them. If possible, they should keep themselves busy on their side, which is cheaper for everyone.

Several governments in the Western world run recruitment programs on a continuous basis, in which they try to find talented hackers, young and smart programmers, as soon as possible, long before they go to university. Real pilots do not want to play with "video games" when operating a military drone, and real spies do not want to hack the servers of a target government while staring at computer monitors all day long. This requires different personalities, although interestingly, psychologists working for the American air force revealed that the results of actions carried out with drones have the same effect on pilots sitting in front of the monitor as their fellow servicemen working on real airplanes.

To find suitable recruits, secret service agencies, the military, and law enforcement agencies regularly attend security and hacker conferences. People in hacker communities and the regular audience at conferences and meetings have various opinions about their presence. The status quo depends a lot on how the reputation of the organization concerned is judged in a given period, determined by press news and leaked information. At DEF CON, a hacker conference in Las Vegas with a long tradition, the game "Spot the fed" was announced back in the 1990s, which – to the pleasure of the hackers – did not earn the FBI's recognition, to say the least. In the game, conference attendees had to spot the secret service agents hidden among them. Those who did really well received a T-shirt saying "I spotted the fed!" while the agent could return to the office with a T-shirt that read "I am the fed!"

To boost recruitment results, the British government even launched a program in which they tried to hunt for young people good at video console games, and without a diploma, for military and secret service agency work. Young people are also attracted to this exciting work through advertisements placed in video games such as Tom Clancy's *Rainbow Six* and *Need for Speed*. There were competitions like The Cyber Security Challenge UK, where first prize was a university course with a value of £100,000 or a job opportunity at the GCHQ cybersecurity center. It is undeniable that more and more young people aged between 12 and 18 choose this modern form of defending their homeland even while they are still at school.

My parents always had German Boxer dogs. The breed's typical flat snout and watchful eyes might fool you if you didn't know these nice and friendly dogs. In short: if we looked at them – and this is important – they seemed to be the toughest guys in the street. In reality, they were quite scared of most things, but just as in the case of professional soldiers, you couldn't see it. Once when I was walking the two of them on a foggy early morning, we got into an unexpected situation. The dogs saw a swaying human body moving toward them in the fog. Almost at the same time, the man noticed them too, and then everyone stopped. The dogs began to growl because they were really scared, the human form tensed, and leaned forward a bit. Nobody moved. What really made me smile was that if any of them had made a suspicious move, the other would have run away. But nobody understood the other's motive, they were unable to imagine themselves in the other's place because the fog was influencing not only their vision but also their thinking. The situation was resolved by communication, I talked to the man and everybody moved on, humans and dogs alike.

That is why another crucial element of the puzzle – i.e. the motive – is so important in cyberspace too. The motive for stealing data or attacking IT systems. Many dismiss this important element, thinking they know what motivates a hacker, but they are usually wrong. Around the eighties and nineties, or even during the early 2000s, we had a general view of hackers. A spotty little kid in the basement, eating mummy's donuts, and at nights when there is nothing interesting on TV he breaks into systems to stalk there for his own amusement. This easily digestible and absolutely logical perception is still held by many people even today, regardless of whether they are good at IT or not: "A hacker is a pipsqueak with glasses, a young little evil-doer. But no worries, he will outgrow it." Yet the group of hackers has broadened, and their motives have changed completely over the roughly 20 years since this way of thinking was born. The representation of classical hackers in the full hacker population has shrunk to about 5-10%, and this number is continuously decreasing. The rest has been filled up by IT specialists who have grown up in the meantime and realized that they could actually make money from their former hobby.

How? For example, they become a white-collar criminal dealing with false banking transactions, money laundering, and other economic crimes in cyberspace. These very successful business fields can even produce a profit amounting to millions of dollars if appropriate actions are carried out, while the chances of getting caught are quite minimal. An adult hacker may for instance be a member of a hacktivist group, who fight for various issues, ideas or from personal belief because, for example, state X launched an offensive in a given country against the population of the Muslim faith, or because it did not launch one. Military techniques range from hacking the Pentagon's site, to exposing people supporting the terrorist Islamic State, to expropriating the personal data of 55 million voters from the electoral system of the Philippines in the first half of 2016. Today, anybody with the occupation of a hacker could even be a soldier, who is paid by the state to enter into the enemy's IT systems during military actions, just like one of the over thirty thousand members of the Chinese hacker armed services. Or they could be a jihadist member, motivated by their interests, principles or the commands of their leaders to shut down certain IT systems: they are saboteurs. Or they could simply be an insane killer who decides that they have to cut the power supply of the USA or a given European country to make everyone else live in darkness like him.

"Then there are cyber mercenaries, who are willing to hack into any system or steal any data for money. Obviously, this is no longer about the joy of theft or the "hacker attitude," but only about financial interests or simply success. Interestingly, serious market analysts such as Gartner predict that by 2020 some 25% of companies will rely on the help of such mercenaries in the growing cyber arms race to be able to store their data – or even to obtain that of others."

A fired employee, who is offended because he was dismissed unlawfully, would like to cause damage while he still has access to the systems. This can even take on extreme forms, as in the case of Vitek Boden who intruded into Queensland's computerized waste management system in Australia; he was the former employee of the firm who had originally installed it, and tried to take over control of the system on 50 occasions until he succeeded, and released 246,000 gallons of uncleaned wastewater into local parks, rivers, and even the territory of Hyatt Regency. According to the representative of the local environmental protection authority, as a result of the contamination aquatic life died out, rivers turned black, and the stink was unbearable for inhabitants. One single employee dismissed... During 2015–2016 a hacktivist group from Syria broke into the industrial systems of an unknown water purification plant, referred to as Kemuri Water Company in the reports, and changed the composition of the chemicals used for purification several times.

We have all surely attended a meeting, a negotiation or community event where we were bored to death. There is no shame in admitting it, just an unpleasant feeling. It is not by chance that we usually do not talk about this, it is a taboo and a secret. Before modern communication tools appeared, for example, I used to amuse myself by writing poems on boring themes, in my head or on paper. Here is one of them, which I composed at a commercial meeting regarding an economic concept that seemed annoying even after several hearings:

"Lost in the dark woods,
Wearing suit and sharp boots,
A manager is wandering,
Missing the days of partnering.
He is all alone and full of fears,
Is that an owl or a wolf he hears?
Bushes rustling, something is chargin',
Too late now! It's the Direct Margin..."

Well, activities like this have been transformed due to the emerging IT systems of the 21st century, and have thus changed us as well. Let's imagine a meeting on Friday afternoon in an office building with glass walls, during which the manager discusses his ideas relating to next week's tasks with six to eight employees. Some of the colleagues find the boss's talk to be uninteresting but, knowing him, they choose to keep quiet – no problem, they will have a good talk about him in the canteen afterward.

Nowadays they don't have to wait until the meeting ends, or write a poem about what the boss says: participants can immediately share their opinions with each other on their laptops or smartphones while listening to the boss's words during the meeting – all they have to watch out for is their facial expression.

It matters what we say, to whom, and, of course, how. Since the beginning of human history we have differentiated between what everyone can hear from our words, and what only a couple of people may know. We prefer to share our everyday intimate details with just a few people, but there are also events in life when we think the opposite, and want as many people to know as possible.

This desire has been limited by various factors for tens of thousands of years. When time – life – is full of hunting, it can be quite risky to stop and chew the fat with the partner by our side, because a wolf might sneak up on us. Yet a community can only be construed as a community as soon as, and so long as, its members are all aware of what has happened to each other. That is why gossip emerged tens of thousands of years ago, and we thus regard it as one of the pillars of social order.

When the strongest, most skillful, and smartest of ancient communities came to prominence based on their capabilities, and gained influence and assets later on, they started to regulate this common knowledge by making declarations, rules, laws, orders, and canons, that further strengthened their existing power. Governing circles ruled from the top, and their top-down communication – and thus their position stabilized by such communication – could rarely be questioned or weakened by grassroots crowds. Rarely, but then to a great extent: when complaints and indignation not channeled into the top-down communication system rose so much that they could not be borne anymore, it often led to riots and revolutions. Most of these incidents were nevertheless unsuccessful because appropriate resources could not be mobilized for the relevant purposes.

The western public sphere in today's sense was born in European cafés sometime in the 18th century. Yet the elite's personal exchange of information collapsed during the 20th century, when mass media emerged. An endless series of reflections were written down, giving cause for concern due to their manipulative nature, while technology was not idle either. New tools were created, but above all, what really laid the foundation for the development of a new public sphere was the spread of the Internet. In the early 21st century community pages appeared, and, as a consequence of their massive popularity, we can talk today about the "informal turn," a change in the public system following the change in the public structure. The greatest achievement of the process is the elastic, ever-changing informal publicity machine, involving an increasing number of people producing increasingly more content.

In the film *Monty Python and the Holy Grail*, by the excellent British comedy group Monty Python, two peasants working on the fields of ancient Britannia respond as follows to King Arthur's question about who their local ruler is: "I told you. We're an anarcho-syndicalist commune. We take it in turns to act as a sort of executive officer for the week. But all the decisions of that officer have to be ratified at a special biweekly meeting." What is funny in this sketch is that in an unrealistic situation, today's way of thinking is put in the mouth of a man who lived hundreds of years ago. While back then only a few hundred farmers used to seethe discretely at the squire's high taxes, to protect their family or land, Web 2.0 arranges the opinions of hundreds of thousands and millions of people into systems in less than a second. This self-organized grassroots communication differs from governed top-down processes mainly in terms of volume.

Another difference is that whereas the latter, a means of power, communicates in vertical systems from the top to the bottom, social media mainly does so horizontally at the level of groups side by side. This is not unlike disgruntled peasants in a small village, airing their petty grievances while the landlord is away; provided that there are only two hundred of them, rather than two thousand. The simultaneous real-time disagreement of such masses can be heard at the top level, and the participants know that. The other side of the coin is that since these masses are organized at the same level, strong connections are less likely to emerge within the core of the organization – what is more, it is easier to deliberately weaken various interest groups from above, e.g. from political powers.

The existence of this phenomenon, i.e. the informal turn, and its processes, leave their mark on today's communities. The number of those who communicate simultaneously creates group characteristics that did not exist before. Posterity will have to consider its positive and negative consequences, but what we already know is that among other things they create a false sense of community. Through our friends we can be anyone, and we feel as if we were more and more similar to each other, although it is really only our habits that become more similar, as they spread more quickly within communities by means of trends and opinions that suddenly become very popular.

In the former small village, old and young, wise and stupid, beautiful and ugly lived together – i.e. most human communities were made up of different groups typical of the given region. Today's groups are not like this: on social media pages anyone can quickly find those who, just like them, enjoy both Rachmaninoff and spinach, and so groups of individuals who live in different parts of the world, but share the same interest or values, are formed worldwide. We are connected to each other not through our limits but through our opportunities.

We often shut down the computer or plug in our mobile phone charger, clutching our head: "I was online for an hour, but I didn't do what I was supposed to do." The number of possibilities is ever-growing, it is hard to enter social media sites or portals while also remaining on track, there are various impulses and we are not used to such volumes. Facilitating decision making has thus become a separate branch of business. In the same way that we recommend a good local bakery to our neighbor, Facebook, Google, and YouTube recommend acquaintances, events, and music – or even a bakery – to us.

Recommendations have risen from the personal micro level to the macro one, while the company winks at us: look, your friends go to this café too! The border between advertisement and recommendation is becoming blurred because I see how many of my friends have liked a given page recommended to me by the social media company.

Corporate communication is organized and governed in a top-down direction, but for business purposes it seems as if they were organized from the bottom to the top. Companies want to be our friends, with products being our family members. Giant corporations know very well that virtuality not only makes the emergence and spread of the informal and hidden possible, but may also accelerate them. They realize this and they react accordingly, because what is interesting for today's public is not that it is virtual but that it is not an officially governed space.

Parallel to the emergence of the informal public, network knowledge is being established. Network knowledge is not a new phenomenon: Guanxi, a central idea in Chinese civilization and a traditional concept of the complex system of networks between individuals and smaller groups from an economic, political, and social perspective, draws on similar reactions.

As early as ancient times, there were lots of connections, but accessing them required significantly more effort than today: they could only learn about the current status of their society if they were present in its locality. Today we can access the internal structure of any system anywhere more easily. Two clicks, and we can see what is happening on the other side of the world, using the live and completely personal channels of YouTube or Facebook. I regularly play an online game, to which I added several hundreds of new Facebook friends. The other day I was surprised to see that one of my unknown fellow players notified me of the live streaming on his Facebook page. I clicked on it, and two seconds later I found myself in a car running on another continent, party to somebody's wife singing modern hits in the passenger seat. I even followed the live stream for a while. Today, in the age of much more data and electronically documented networks, we must face the fact that some of our relationships are "laid open", i.e. they can be accessed, watched, and analyzed from any part of the world, but in return the system also discloses some things about itself. When researching the whole thing – which is more than the sum of its parts – society is researching itself. While the details of a given person and their relations are revealed, their activity on the web also enables them to gain knowledge of the system, whereby they contribute to the formation of the network itself. As soon as we observe the system, we also interfere with it and change it.

The effect of the informal turn is huge, and yet it has not led to the extinction of gossip or the break-down of taboos, and this will never happen. On the contrary, as members of the virtual public we see the difference more clearly: what we can say only in words and, especially in private, what real secrets are.

My friend's child developed a rather annoying habit at the age of two: When nobody was watching him, he would secretly take some of the objects deemed important by his family members, break them apart, and hide the sections in different points of the house, then stand in front of his family, shoulders lifted slightly, and ask with his eyebrows raised: "Where?" Everyone knew this meant that some important object was lost, and was waiting for somebody to find its hidden pieces.

In the wealth of information, taboos, and secrets that make up cyberspace, we perceive a closer relationship between inaccessible information, secrets, and the hackers' primary motivation of curiosity. Whether ethical or not, if a hacker comes up against a wall, its mere presence annoys him, he doesn't like it. He wants to go through it to see what is on the other side.

Hackers generally have a strong sense of justice, or some motivation deemed to be a sense of justice. This is not a Robin Hood type sense of justice, but rather, "Yes I will go in there," "Yes I have the right to do so," and "Everyone should see everything." In most cases, hackers have something to prove to themselves: they can enter, hack, and open up the system. It is not by coincidence that lock-picking demonstrations are recurring themes at hacker conferences, and participants are also able to try their hand. I would like to add that those who have tried to see how many seconds it takes to open a traditional lock without difficulty after one hour's practice, will look at door locks, especially their own, in a completely different way. Protecting information technology systems is often quite similar.

Many different attitudes can be observed in the behavior of hackers. Some say the reason they take things apart is to see how they work, and then they put them back together to make them better, and more secure. Others take things apart just because, and they leave them that way. They can come from many different groups in society, they can be wealthy, poor, geniuses or less so, experts only within a given area. The urge to gain access is very strong, and while we cannot really call it an instinct, this is part of every hacker's basic motivation.

Kevin Mitnick was an active hacker in the US in the 1980s and 1990s. He was able to hack into the systems of virtually all of the large global technology corporations. Though he was pursued by all of the law enforcement and secret service agencies in the USA, he was only captured after being on the run for many years and after many embarrassing blunders from the police and secret service agencies. Mitnick consistently alleged that he had never published or sold any of the information he obtained. His court hearing exposed a series of regulatory deficiencies in the US justice system, and the trial was essentially conducted amid non-existent IT laws and vague accusations. His incarceration was accompanied by vociferous "Free Kevin" campaigns, with activists calling for his release. The justice system feared his abilities as the "top hacker" to such an extent that he was even banned from using a computer or a telephone for a lengthy period. Apple's co-founder Steve Wozniak became a good friend of the hacker over the years, and after the ban was lifted he personally and gladly handed over an early model of the Apple computer. Following his imprisonment he set up a security company, and to this day he provides consulting services for companies, including those which were previously victims of his hacks.

Aside from his incredible technological expertise in the tools of that era, one of Mitnick's most important weapons was "social engineering", i.e. his ability to manipulate people, or, as the title of one of his books reads: *The Art of Deception*. On his way home from work and amid a huge snowfall and heavy traffic he called the Motorola cell phone manufacturing department from a pay-phone, and using only manipulative methods he managed to persuade them to send him the source code and designs for the company's newest cell phone. Mitnick's methods were precursors to today's deception letters and telephone calls targeting staff at companies, and well illustrate the almost 100% effectiveness even now of exploiting human weaknesses.

One of the most significant aspects of every cyber attack, data leak or vilification, and also the most difficult to identify, is the motivation of the attacker and what lies behind it. The curiosity of a hacker is to all intents and purposes a scalable motive. The big question surrounding the topic of hackers leads us to explore issues such as curiosity, freedom fighting, heroism, and provocation: is it not simply that the hacker lies to himself that he is exposing something for the public good, when in actual fact he is doing it in his own interest, and not for money but to be famous?

An age-old problem of the malicious hacker community is that they are unable to hold themselves back and always want to boast. Isn't it annoying to hack into the most classified systems within the Pentagon, but then be unable to tell anyone how much of a genius you are?

Many of them want to be heroes, or at least want to tell their friends and buddies what they have done, but if more than one person knows then this triggers a snowball effect, culminating sooner or later in exposure – the eternal hacker dilemma. The police and secret service agencies have been helped in exposing many hackers by "loose tongues," i.e. simple human weaknesses, not by some super high-tech solution.

Keeping quiet is not a problem for professional hackers. White-collar cybercriminals will never boast of their "success" because they carried out an assignment for which they earned their money. This is a change related to personality. And do not forget that their clients know what they are capable of, meaning that their relevant need can be satisfied. Since society itself is made up of more and more groups, hacker motives have also become too varied to determine exactly what has happened and for what reason.

In addition to the above, another drive is also worth discussing: power. A new kind of power is emerging, in the control of IT over systems. In this regard, citizens do not have anything to fear from their bank, but from hackers who have a hold over their bank or bank account. The hacking attacks against the Society for Worldwide Interbank Financial Telecommunication (SWIFT), published during 2016, resulted in losses of several hundreds of millions of dollars to banks and investors. These attacks clearly showed that economic powers with money are insufficient when a hacker or a group of hackers take control of an IT system that represents money.

This possibility offers so much power to hackers, it is difficult to refuse. It must be wonderful when somebody feels like the king of the world – and the media even takes this heroism one stage further, showing the hacker's life and activity to be extremely exciting. And I'm not principally thinking of the hacker played by Hugh Jackman in the movie *Swordfish*, who is forced to break into the Department of Defense while a gun is held to his temple and a pretty woman "satisfies" him under the table, even though he only has 60 seconds to do the job. Not just because people usually do not break into the Department of Defense within a minute just by kicking down the front door, but because hackers generally do not look like Hugh Jackman, their enemies are not like John Travolta, and few have extra "assistance" under the table while working. The public perception of hacking is diversified by the fact that the activity itself, or opinions about the information gained and published this way, is different at various social levels. Edward Snowden, a former employee of the US secret service who leaked its biggest secrets, is considered a hero and a traitor by equal numbers, and even this image is not fixed but changes constantly. People approve of, rather than reject, the hacker actions of the Anonymous group that were launched against the terror of the Islamic State.

While hackers draw a self-image of themselves ranging from a hero to a hacker specialist, and society judges them in completely different ways, with many still thinking of them as some kind of ringleaders, they are often nothing more than instruments. Economic or political powers are at work in cyberspace as well – this is where a hacker can become an instrument of spying, intelligence, attacks or anything else that the authority wants to achieve.

CHAPTER 3

HOUSTON, OUR SECRECY PARADIGMS ARE SHIFTING!

*"Hi Computer, last time I saw you,
you were this big, and you,
little Data were so small..."*

Astronomers say that in the past ten years their field has made great advances because they have so much data to analyze, so much information is arriving from their telescopes placed outside the Earth's airspace that they can only process it with modern IT capacities. A new group of information consumers has appeared in the meantime that they had not counted on: Not astronomers, not even amateur ones, but simply people who can create new information from public data, collected and made available using their own devices and computers; people who can, more importantly, with their enthusiasm and interest, find new planets.

Today, mankind is producing data in quantities that has to be processed by machines to make it consumable for us, so that we can draw conclusions from it. Although the economic drivers of modern consumer society have already created big data analysis programs for stock exchange, corporate governance or transport management systems, a number of other important areas (such as general healthcare or everyday activities like eating, shopping, news consumption, and organizing tasks) have yet to see such solutions, we still rely on human routines here. But we don't have to wait too long for the arrival of such analyzing capacities and devices, and by offering us the best options, and pre-digesting information, these systems will transform our lives to the extent that mobile phones and smart devices have transformed our communication and our memories. However there is something else they will do: they will increase our vital dependence on IT systems and on the information stored in them, and will enhance our expectations of the content, availability, and reliability of the information. So just as we can now press the call button on our phone and expect to talk to the chosen person, in the future it will be the same with the gluten content of the food choices offered to us by machines, or when determining the optimal time to go to bed.

This is why it is important to understand the challenges facing our comprehension of the content, the confidentiality, and the authenticity of information, as well as our principles. Let me walk you through these paradigm shifts.

1. The emergence of networks. When computers worked in isolation, independently, they were less exposed to security issues. They were independent of one another, they did not communicate with one another, they could not infect one another or exchange information, so a virus or a hacker could not inflict too much damage on them. In the 1980s for example, those happy peaceful times for home computers, there wasn't a single virus hiding among the thousands of Commodore 64 games I owned. Becoming part of a network and starting to communicate was a big step forward; as our possibilities grew, so did our problems, as is usually the case with mankind.

2. The second step of such magnitude is the growing of capacities. We have smart phones now, and mobile devices. These are actually miniature computers whose portability and enhanced capacities have turned the playing field upside down. Twenty years ago, computers used to sit on desks and networks ended in walls. All neatly ordered and transparent. Twenty years ago in a television ad by Swedish communication company Geab, we see three men sitting in a sauna. Suddenly a mobile phone starts ringing, and lifting his hand, the Asian man on the left starts talking into the ring on his finger in Chinese. When he is finished, he looks at the others with the satisfaction of having a technological edge. Seconds later, a tooth of the middle-aged

man in the middle starts ringing. The man puts down the paper he is reading, touches his tooth to answer the call with a single tap, and says in US English, "Hi Bob, 50 million? Go for it, Bob! Bye!" He looks proudly at the Asian man and with a smug look on his face he returns to his paper. The Scandinavian guy in the corner, clearly unsure of what he has just seen, is anxious. Then leaning slightly to one side, he starts to make rattling and whistling noises to the wall in the sauna. When the other two look at him questioningly, he simply says, "I'm getting a fax!" While a mobile phone hidden in a ring or a tooth was downright ridiculous in 1996, in 2016 we can no longer say it is impossible. Portable and mobile devices have turned the tables upside down, and the companies delivering the technology have tried to adapt to this. Self-defending networks and border protection appeared in the security industry. But this still wasn't enough. All too soon it turned out that the border or boundary we could protect does not exist. Boundaries are everywhere where there are computers. With a mobile in our pockets we have pocketed the network as well, so the question of "where?" has become moot. Of course, there is still a network and also border protection, since there are still systems that require central protection. The networks, however, have opened up due to the increased number of mobile phones and the capacities of processors enhanced to a degree that already has a major impact on us as people and on our protection.

3. Now we have arrived at a dramatic increase in the quantity of data, when we talk about zetabytes in internet traffic. On the other hand, the SI units introduced in the early 1990s for these

bytes will soon be used up and we'll have to come up with the next ones. The SI units already had the prefixes giga and tera in addition to the common kilo and mega when the system was standardized in 1960. The next two steps, the prefixes peta (10^{15}) and exa (10^{18}) were added in 1975, but we'll soon be finished with them as well, so 1991 saw the addition of zeta and yotta to the measurement system. By the way, yotta, 10^{24}, looks like this when written in numbers: 1 000 000 000 000 000 000 000 000, which does not even fit the screen of traditional computers, but we will use it all the same. So we'd better get used to seeing the abbreviations ZB (ZetaByte) and YB (YottaByte).

We have to store this immense amount of data somewhere, so storage systems and the IT systems built around them have become increasingly complex: today we are already talking about 5D storage, using nanostructured glass, the theoretical life expectancy of which is about 14 billion years. Miniaturization is also undergoing a data storage revolution: 2016 saw the birth of a memory unit suitable for mass production, which has a diameter of 3 cm, a weight of 1 gram and a capacity of 512 gigabytes (i.e. suitable for storing about 100 HD films). Such solutions will fundamentally change the methods of data storage from one minute to the next. Right now, millions of pictures are taken every second all over the world, even 360 degree (look-around) video content has appeared, not to mention other databases. And it is in this vast amount of data that we have to find the problem: the security issue, the hole, the access problems. Security experts or law enforcement bodies often try to find a few megabytes of malignant information or program among several millions of bytes, and the realistic chances of success are millions to one.

These technological revolutions are resulting in a paradigm shift concerning secrets: Will we be able to spot the hacker hunting down our secrets, the data stealing application, or the sensitive information leaving our computers amid the mass of information, where everything takes place in a fraction of a second in a network that connects everything with everything else? South-East Asia has more than 400 indigenous species of mosquito, including ones that can only be spotted in a museum exhibition display cabinet with a magnifying glass. Now imagine this mosquito as you try to spot it atop the latest Chinese high-speed train at 267.8 mph as it flies over you, and you're trying to catch it with a Coke bottle. It is no coincidence that in this region, the saying goes, "It's like trying to find a needle in the ocean." And that's what we can expect.

If we try to comprehend the basis of a secret in this fast, complicated, and gigantic modern digital world, then we realize that answers to the questions of "what?" "from whom?" and "when?" may increase our chances of being successful. If someone obtains the information and knows what to do with it, how to trade it, then they can create secrets and specific information: the content created this way will gain new value, which is valid for a limited period of time. The shell over secrets is beginning to crack open, we can already say that content, time, and source are all integral parts of the formula for a secret. Its value can be determined based on what it contains, whom it comes from and when it was created.

CHAPTER 4

THE TRAGEDY OF THE POOR ENCRYPTOR AND THE UPPERCLASSIFICATION OF DATA

Does anyone actually know which information is important?

The short answer is: no. Because it's not the information itself that's important but the way or the process through which it becomes a secret, how it is evaluated by the various players, and what value it will have at a given point in time. This is why the classification of data is practically incomprehensible for private individuals and is a difficult task even for organizations: they often do not even know what kind of data they have...

Just imagine that vast amounts of data are collected about who crosses which border of which country, and when. This database allows us to draw some basic conclusions, we can establish, for example, if the number of visitors from a given country goes up year-to-year. This, however, is not a secret per se, it would even be worth sharing with anybody who could draw important and useful conclusions due to their profession or knowledge. The moment a terrorist act happens or a war breaks out however, all of a sudden this information becomes much more important, the events make them a secret. It was not a secret before, so the context changes its value, and, what's more, the context appreciates it to a massive extent.

Since it's very difficult to determine our relationship to this timeframe and context, and to the real value of the information, we often do not try to protect our data, we encrypt it. What sounds at first like a good solution, like a wall, is fundamentally a different kind of protection. If you want to understand the difference between the two ways of thinking then imagine two kids in a sand pit. One of the kids can see that the other has a purple plastic bucket. He likes the bucket, so approaches the other kid to take it away from him. The one with the purple bucket makes a ditch around himself in the sand, and fills it with mud to keep the other kid away. If he comes too close, the kid with the bucket might start to throw sand in his eyes, or turn his back but keep an eye on the other kid to see when he tries to snatch his bucket, and to react if he does. This is our defense strategy today when it comes to data protection. A logical step away from this strategy in the future could be to encrypt more and more things: the kid may not even see that the other one has a purple bucket. Even if he does spot it, he may not realize that it is a purple bucket. Simply put, this is an entirely new defensive principle. If, say, we use a password-storing application and we store all our passwords there, they will be encrypted. That's why it can end up on the internet, there's no problem as it's encrypted. We won't be happy if someone has it, and we try to protect it, to prevent them from getting it, from snatching our purple bucket, but basically we don't care as it has been encrypted anyway. The EU data protection regulation taking effect in 2018 will sanction organizations from which data is stolen if the data was not encrypted.

The question, however, is whether the right to encryption is a fundamental human right, i.e. the right to prevent others accessing our information. Mankind hasn't yet been faced with the general manifestation of this problem: we can solve these things by devoting enough time and energy. The problem itself used to be limited in general to criminals, people who were intent on hiding their data, but the authorities could always access the information sooner or later. Then secrets causing headaches for larger organizations started to appear as well. Take the case of Ricky McCormick in the US, aged 41, whose body was found by the FBI back in 1999. In 2011 the FBI opted for a rather unusual way of involving the public in solving the case that had been a mystery for 12 years. After their own expert group failed to come up with results, the public was asked to help crack the cipher they found in the man's pocket, which might shed light on the circumstances of the homicide. The strange cipher, which the FBI's code-breakers maintain they have never seen anything like before, has been a subject of criticism and mystery ever since.

In the same year a number of legal and expert debates were sparked by the case of Ramona Fricosu, who was charged with child pornography and ordered, at the request of the district attorney, to decode her computer, on the grounds that this prevented police from solving the case as they were unable to reveal her secrets. At the same time, in another case in the US, the court did not order the defendant to disclose his password, saying that by decoding his computer the defendant may be obliged to produce evidence harming his own defense, essentially testifying against himself, which is forbidden by law. In both cases the law enforcement authorities and the prosecution were unable to decrypt the computers, which is why they turned to the court, and in one case the information was allowed to remain the secret of the defendant. A few years later the infamous Apple vs FBI case reared its head, in which the technology company refused to meet the court's request and decrypt the mobile phone of one of the perpetrators of the San Bernardino terrorist attack as requested by the FBI. In this case, time was also a factor since the original owner of the phone was no longer alive to reveal the password.

When it comes to encryption, any combination of the situations above can happen. After 17 years of loyal service, a former sergeant at the Philadelphia police department will remain in custody until he reveals the password to the encryption on his computer; although he has not been formally charged with anything yet, it is alleged that his computer could contain information related to child pornography. Once again, the point is that the authorities cannot access people's personal information, it's there, they are aware of its existence, but they cannot open it. The secret, whatever it may be, is lying on a desk at the police station like some annoying, closed little box.

So we have arrived at an era when technology companies, seeking to earn consumers' trust, have hurried to the defense of individuals trying to protect their privacy, and left it up to their customers to decide about their secrets and whether to disclose them or not. And this raises the following question: if petty criminals and big terrorist organizations alike can hide whatever information they choose to hide, and they can easily and successfully do so at any time, then what are our law enforcement bodies supposed to do? Should they just ask the criminal nicely to hand the information over? And if they get a negative response, they should quietly thank them for cooperating and simply move on? Or should they put everyone in jail until they confess their secrets? And what about the content of those who are no longer alive?

A priest knows the content of a confession, but Apple does not. If someone confesses today that they murdered three people, but the conversation is encrypted in a way that even Microsoft or Google is unable to access it, then there is no 'priest': even the secret service agencies and government bodies are unable to access it.

The situation is further complicated by the fact that if you witness something in the cyberworld today that you believe to be illegal (for example, you become an eye- or an ear-witness to a criminal act) and you want to report it, this will be tough to do because there is no proper forum for digital eyewitness evidence, and the application in cyberspace of the fundamental rights we know from our physical space is still in its infancy.

In the cybersecurity industry, new secrecy-related issues are raised every day. I must hear at least three times a week: "I could tell you, but then I'd have to kill you." Although this saying goes back centuries in literary traditions, I believe that in light of the above it's time for a rethink: 'Before I tell you, I have to kill you.'

Yet the bigger problem with encryption is that not even the authorities or the state are able to access the full content of communication encrypted to protect the privacy of users. They are unable to tap conversations in the investigation stage of proceedings and are unable to defuse the activities of hostile spies or terrorists. They cannot even ascertain whether their basic assumptions regarding the person targeted (suspicion of terrorism or drug trafficking, for instance) are true, and whether the investigation and the monitoring can continue. At the moment it seems it will be up to the individuals and the technology companies to decide who can listen in on or monitor interpersonal communication. Deciding whether to allow the police to see their communication does not present a major problem for criminals, but for the vast majority of citizens it is an issue, even just to decide which organization they should allow insight into their privacy. Sure, let counterintelligence in, we aren't spies after all. Let counter-terrorism in, we aren't terrorists after all. We aren't criminals, so let the police in too. Since we don't commit tax fraud, we can obviously let the tax authority have a look at our secret information too. Since we pay properly for water and electricity, why not give information to these service providers as well?

I guess some of you were stopped in your thoughts while reading just the names of the first few organizations. But no matter how deep ordinary people let these organizations into their privacy, they should always remember two things: the hunger of the state and other organizations for information is simply insatiable. We should remember that information has never commanded such great power as it does in the 21st century. It seems that the various organizations, the state in particular, are not able to protect the information they store today, and will not be able to do so in the future either. 2015 and 2016 saw a series of hacker attacks and successful thefts of personal data belonging to tens of millions of government employees in the USA alone. Let's remember what Gartner predicted: by 2020, those whom we entrust with our data will not be able to protect 75% of it.

As the credits start to roll at the end of *Star Wars,* Farmer Joe shakes his head in the movie theater: "Well, I just cannot believe all that."

So there has to be a solution to data security issues as well. If I wanted to carry on Farmer Joe's train of thought: "There are so many clever people working for you, solve that data security thing." The good news, of course, is that, "We *can* explain." Data security is guaranteed by regulations, processes, and solutions preventing unauthorized access. When drafting and implementing them, we need to answer the question of **what needs protection?** Not only the data and the information itself, but also the forms and carrier devices, and their locations, whether they are stored on paper, electronically or in human brains.

The next question is: **what does it need protection from?** How confidential is the information, how decisive is it to another piece of data or information, and how is the information to be protected made available? And finally, **in what way does it need protection?** Once we know what we need to protect and from what, we can start drawing up a strategy.

The human risk is a key element in this strategy. Negative personal traits, financial or other problems, the conflicts and problematic situations of staff, are not a threat on their own, but they are when in the direct vicinity of a secret. Of course, every step we take to protect these secrets apparently violates the freedom of information, but let's dig a bit deeper.

The "what needs protection?" question is not so easy to answer as you might think. Data can be personal, special or organizational, and we can establish several subcategories within these. There are a few (typically personal) pieces of information which can more or less be regarded as sensitive, e.g. the sexual orientation or the medical history of an individual. Yet with such sensitive information it often depends on the situation to determine whether they should be treated as secret or not. Suppose the law says we are not authorized to be informed about whether another person is ill or not. People in a hospital, for instance, are all ill, they already know that about one another, since they are treated at the same place. People in a given department of the hospital will have similar illnesses, and that too is obvious to the other patients. Patients undergoing a particular treatment may also have the same illness. So, exactly what, how, and when should hospital patients hide from one another, and how should staff behave to make sure that secrets remain with their owners?

To add yet another twist, we must understand that both private individuals and organizations find it rather hard to identify exactly which parts of their information require protection. To give you an idea, it's worth considering how hard most people find it to categorize the data to be protected. Resolving the seemingly simple "secret/not secret" dilemma is hard because we ask ourselves: who is this a secret for and when? For example, communication intended for the members of management is supposed to be a secret at what level? And within what timeframe? And even if we specify all this and implement it, how are we going to comply with it or enforce it? What are the "conventional" social and organizational rules on keeping secrets anyway? Not to mention more complicated data protection categories such as classified, confidential, top secret, secret, restricted, etc. In order for such categories of secret to make sense so that we can actually use them, we need to know the laws, regulations, and internal rules applying to the given organization.

The laws classifying data movement within governmental or law enforcement organizations vary from country to country, though they are based on similar principles. I would love to say that in 2015 the researchers of the University of Willsempthon were able to teach the above logic to male savanna vervets, aged five to eight, under laboratory conditions, and that therefore it should not be a problem for human beings either, but to the best of my knowledge no such experiment took place and I have serious doubts concerning humans as well. This is simply far too much and far too complex for us to have a comprehensive overview.

The icing on the cake is that most such categories may be rendered meaningless when they move among organizations working in different fields and are almost certain to cease existing when they cross sectors or social borders. The only exception to this may be classified state secrets protected by law, but such categories may also fall outside sensitive data when reaching certain borders. And of course, a lot depends on who declared what to be a secret. The issue of classifying the information to be protected and the interpretation of laws or rules may reach such complicated levels that legal and IT experts and legislators end up having debates on them for days, weeks or even years. Conferences and meetings are organized on the issue, and on top of all this, the classifications that work properly in theory cause feasibility and technology problems on a daily basis in practice, and make procurement more difficult, meaning that they often get ignored or interpreted more "loosely."

In private life classifying data is even more difficult. In our everyday life we do not employ such methods to categorize information and we do not rank them under official classifications. You are highly unlikely to hear the sentence, for example, "Son, your mother's birthday present is strictly confidential information with restricted access," in most families. But that does not mean that private individuals do not have sensitive data and information, and the thing that is most difficult to protect: secrets.

It seems worthwhile to say a few words about the notion of "data." You cannot really back IT experts, mathematicians or engineers into a corner by asking them what data is. Most of the time they will rattle off several neat definitions, ones they can work with really well in their own fields. Yet the man in the street is not in such an easy position. Many people do not even realize that they have data at all, or that when they search Google or post something on Facebook, they are actually transferring data. What is more, they probably do not realize that their data will end up in a gigantic data center at the other end of the globe within seconds. Data can, therefore, have different statuses. As IT experts try to define it: data can be in motion, at rest or in use, and it will be treated, used, and managed in different ways accordingly. So if we try to look at the issue from a protection point of view, the sensitive data even of individuals can be interpreted in at least two stages. Stage one is the user himself who has to, or rather should, decide which data is sensitive, important to him, and requiring protection. In other words, what his secret is and what level that secret has. Stage two takes us to the realm of IT systems and their creators, it's the software and the hardware that has to provide adequate protection for data, the level of which we have already defined. In addition to many other technologies, this includes protection against viruses, firewalls, and encrypting devices. Seeing the desperate look on my face, my dentist usually says at this point, "We are nearly done now," but he already said that twice during the treatment. I would love to say the same, but I won't lie. Alas, the hardest part is yet to come.

The real protection of the secret has already failed at level one, i.e. at the point where the user classifies his own secrets himself. It is no coincidence that in the cybersecurity profession the user is often defined as problem number one, and it is a standing joke that if you remove users from an IT system it will all of a sudden start to function properly, hence the expression: "User error." Perhaps this is why security experts often recommend that we encrypt everything (the entire content of storage hosts for example,) making everything a secret, so that we would not have to think about what is less and what is more sensitive data. This is how we end up in a situation where we encrypt each and every communication (even ones like "Hello, I'm back from the garden,") and that's what annoys the police, counter-terrorism organizations, and governments in general. But let's get back to the data.

Data has another unfortunate characteristic, it is not static or stable, and is in almost constant movement. A few pieces of natural information such as the date and place of birth remain the same, but our credit card data or the medication we take will be different all the time. And as we approach the frequently used data of our daily lives, this constant nature disappears accordingly. Protection must follow the changes, but as such information wavers between the various levels of confidentiality, since what is sensitive or should be hidden today will be public tomorrow, static protection cannot be effective either. This raises the question of what exactly it is in the original data that changes? This is typically the problem that IT and cybersecurity experts, and the lawyers of various organizations, are faced with when they try to make classifications. It often takes such data content analysis and classification projects to make companies and organizations realize just how little they know about their own processes as well as the content and the nature of the data created by them. This is hardly surprising as an organization with thousands of people usually works with thousands of processes and several terabytes of data. No wonder therefore that it is downright or nearly impossible to review them, and once we are finished with that job we can start all over again because the business processes have changed, along with all our data. That's why companies tend to focus on processes involving business continuity and on identifying the processes critical to their operation. This usually provides a more manageable set with much fewer processes and much less data to be protected. At the same time it is tricky because if the management of a company focuses on protecting this data only, then they can easily lose sight of less sensitive processes and systems, and this is where hacker attacks are started. There is no point in concentrating solely on the proper functioning of our heart if we can die from a small wound becoming infected.

In 2008, Barclays Bank in the UK was also focusing on protecting its critical banking processes when a hacker, employing the social engineering style manipulation tools we know all too well from Kevin Mitnick, tricked the bank's customer service on the phone into issuing him with a new credit card, which he collected and used to swipe some $20,000 from the account of the bank's CEO. The bank admitted the error in the processes of its telephone customer service and claims "to have learned from its mistakes." Eight years on, the manipulation problem is far from being solved, in fact it has escalated. Hackers these days not only make phone calls, they also write deceptive emails to company managers or their financial representatives. In early 2016, a Belgian bank announced that they had fallen victim to a $78.5 million fraud committed with such a method, and the same thing happened to an Austrian company manufacturing spare parts for planes, which lost $54 million. The FBI says that fraud-based hacks, targeting members of top management, exploit the credulity of staff and management, as well as complicated corporate processes, and have caused losses of $1.2 billion around the globe. In the US this loss amounted to almost $800 million in two years.

Unfortunately, private individuals are lagging behind companies as families do not know "their critical business processes" and do not realize which items of data are indispensable from all the data they need.

Now add the secret-related paradigm shifts to these rather uncertain circumstances: the appearance of nearly infinite networks, the dramatic strengthening of computer capacity, and the increased amounts of data that can be measured in zetabytes, and it is not very hard to see that the fate of our secrets is quite hopeless.

CHAPTER 5

RISK PARALYSIS AND UNFORTUNATE PROTECTION

*I mean, risk analysis
and proportionate protection,
which part can't you
understand?*

Indonesian sci-fi author and poet, Toba Beta, says in one of his books, "When you are dealing with an invisible enemy, use most resources as shield, and a bit as bait." This is what happens when organizations realize that it is a tough job to protect their own data while hacker attacks, and thefts of data and money, are reported on a daily basis. They hide behind their shields and that's when the magical sword is drawn from its sheath: risk analysis. To describe the unconscious driving force behind risk analysis, let me quote the CEO of a European telecommunications company, "The point is to do something... does this count as something?

Let's go for it then." When carrying out a risk analysis, the leaders, operators and staff of organizations will follow one or another standard or practice to weigh, one by one, the risks lurking around them; how likely they are to happen, how frequently they happen, their potential impact, and lots of other factors. Just like with any other system based on self-assessment, here too we meet all too often with the principle that "Every man kindles the fire below his own pot," alongside the stress relieving effects of the attitude, "Nah, nothing will happen anyway, and if it does, we'll muddle through somehow." Simply put: the analysts and the decision-makers often ignore or underestimate many events or effects.

It's interesting to see how the ethical and less-than-ethical hacker community regularly smiles at risk analysis and at the work of the auditors carrying it out, sometimes even making a show of their contempt, saying, "Our dear colleagues keep analyzing this, writing that, ticking off check-lists, and it takes us no more than a few seconds to hack their web server and take their data." Of course it works the other way around as well, among auditors not much credit is given to the image of a provocative hacker with a big mouth, who thinks short-term and does not give a damn about systematic work and discipline.

Suppose the risk analysis has been carried out, the magical sword has been pulled and *ta-dah*: the problematic points have been identified. What follows next is retrieving the magical shield, if you like, from your armaments chest: the risk proportionate protection. Held in high regard by experts, this essentially aligns the necessary security level and technique along with its method to the assessed risk. But the truth is, in reality you can put just about anything from non-existing security to 100% protection behind the slogan of "risk proportionate protection." And companies and businesses use this in any way they can. A competent security expert can use the very same argument for and against a security investment. It all boils down to how seriously you can take that risk and how acceptable the proposed solution is.

And this raises the following question: in what way is the complexity of the given facility connected to the complexity of the protection? Is a bank more complicated than a sewage treatment plant? Or a nuclear plant, a traffic system, a hospital, an airplane or a spaceship? Or a subsystem of public administration, for that matter? The logic of information security does not start with thinking about how complicated it can be to protect a particular system, but what challenges it faces and what the impacts of those challenges might be. It is no coincidence that national leaders and security experts find it so hard, or even impossible, to agree on what counts as critical or vital infrastructure and what doesn't, since a sewage company of minor importance at first glance could become crucial after rainy weather for days on end or after a sudden thaw, while a bakery or a pharmaceutical company could easily find themselves in the same situation during a military coup or a viral crisis for example. Simply put, anything can be vital from a certain point of view. It's a bit like packing for a holiday. What won't we need? What should I leave at home, the umbrella or the painkillers? Contrary to popular belief, successful classification is not, unfortunately, key to the successful protection of a company or organization. Malware programs have been detected at the International Space Station, and in 2013 a US electricity company was brought to its knees by a virus for three weeks, not to mention the successful cyber attacks at countless power plants, military facilities, and banks.

As Winston Churchill put it, "Democracy is the worst form of government, except for all those other forms that have been tried from time to time." The same principle applies when using risk analysis. Since no one has come up with a better general rule, information security is trying to do just the same: focusing on what risks the given person, company, organization or group carries, and given the risks, what protection they can come up with.

A private individual can have a complicated protection system, too: if he saves and encrypts all of his documents, if he updates his anti-virus software at all times, if he changes all his passwords every month, and if he knows what he is doing. This is just as complicated for a private individual as for a company, that protects the data of all of their clients as well as their own processes and information. True, they have to employ a lot of people to do that and it costs more. Yet it is still problematic to categorize what is easy or difficult to protect and why. One aspect to be factored in could be the sensitivity and importance of the data stored, or the operation of critical infrastructure where the risks threatening the data are substantial. In such cases it will be more expensive and more complicated to tackle their protection.

Data can also be classified on the basis of sensitivity; this affects its protection too, as does the critical nature of the system and the data itself. In a nuclear plant, for instance, protecting the numerical information on what temperature it is inside the reactor may not be the most important issue. What we have to be careful about is making sure that the data is measurable and authentic, so that the temperature cannot exceed a given level and nobody can tamper with it, because that could lead to a disaster. In mid-2016 for example, industry media was preoccupied with a malware program named Irongate, which provides a framework in industrial systems for man-in-the-middle attacks, meaning it transmits false data to the operators of a power plant, for example, while being able to manipulate the information from the actual system unnoticed. In this case it is the content of the data that's important, not whether it's there or not, or who can access it from the public. Data, as a basic unit, is therefore a tough question. Most of the time, however, we measure risks according to the form of the data, and the possibilities and levels of access.

On top of all that, the system and the data itself are unfortunately changing all the time. New processes are created, old processes change, and the protection needs rethinking in its entirety; data needs to be re-classified, new data owners need to be designated, since secure operations must be ensured for new processes too. This is not an easy job for companies, which prompts them to provide for more static protection.

An average person, of course, lags behind in security issues, and equally so when it comes to risk analysis. Just as you won't find data classification, categorization of secrets, and the analysis of processes critical to the operation of the family in an average home, you won't find any risk analysis either. It's fair to say that when Dad buys an anti-virus program for the home, he does actually carry out a one-minute risk analysis followed by buying protection proportionate with the risks, but in reality it's more likely to be along the lines of, "My son's computer has been wrecked by a virus," "My neighbor has one too," and "I'm told you need one."

CHAPTER 6

ACCESS DATA MUST NOT FEAR WILL BE GOOD

Rights restricting productivity, intrigue, and heart-stopping secrets

A great friend of mine, Viktor, has a favorite story. One beautiful day, the bell rang. He went to open the gate of the private garden by his apartment building, to find out who it was and what they wanted. By the time he reached the path surrounding the garden, the two visitors, who had just rung the bell, were in the courtyard. When they saw him coming, they broke into a smile and announced: "We have brought the message of the Redeemer, which we would like to pass on to you!" to which Viktor replied, "Ok, but how did you get in?" Doesn't sound too nice, right? Yet we still allow ourselves a smile because we feel that this the appropriate or at least the main question here. That said, few of us are able to focus on basic security issues in such a scenario.

Data protection faces the same quandary. Who can access what data, when, and how? In an ideal world this would be easy to resolve. We could say that someone can only enter a certain place when they actually need to, and they can only access the things that they need to, and only when they need to: the perfect rights management system! ...In theory.

In practice though, things are completely different. Processes change quickly, information and data are needed quickly, and people either get it, or if they don't, then processes slow down or stop – this is not something that anybody wants at an efficient company or organization. Money talks! It suffices to ask a company manager or a restaurant owner. Down to the very last dollar they can tell you how much a minute of downtime costs the organization that they run. The most advanced car manufacturers in the world make a car every one or two minutes! Good luck to the person putting that at risk by slowing down the rights management process: the operations manager would be on them in an instant.

One common experience in information security is that the more easily a given system can be used, the less secure it is. And the more secure it is, the less it can be used. In my experience, staff at companies and organizations demand greater utility from their systems after a while so that they can work efficiently, yet by doing so this impairs the system's level of protection. This general principle can be found in all systems and processes managed by IT, even in those created for security purposes. Admittedly this isn't a new phenomenon: fully armored knights in the Middle Ages had to strike compromises with their protection in order to be able to move their limbs: their armor was separated at the joints and they only wore chainmail underneath, which gave them the freedom they needed to move. It was at these points that enemy soldiers attacked with their swords and arrows. The knights somehow had to see out from their strong armor, which is why there was a small gap cut into the helmet when it was made. So even if nothing could pierce the full battle armor, a thin blade aimed at the joints and the helmet was able to literally apply the *coup de grâce*. This weapon was called a "misericorde," which we could also refer to as the rootkit (software attacking the heart of IT systems) of the knights in the Middle Ages.

So to ensure that we enjoy both protection and versatility, rights management must be introduced as part of a project, which is when we are confronted with rights matrices. These are large databases and software that determine who can access which system, process or data, when, and for what purpose. Rights management systems generally determine the level of access based on the position of the users. These roles change over time (when someone is promoted or made redundant for example) or in a given situation (when we need to substitute for a manager or another colleague) and the systems track them, in theory. The emphasis here is on the "track" and "in theory." It is therefore conceivable that someone has been able to access given information for a certain time, but now should not be allowed access, because they no longer work with it or need it for their job.

This alone creates multi-dimensional matrices that are so complex they become increasingly hard for companies to manage them, despite even medium-sized organizations employing a separate member of staff to monitor processes and manage rights. Even when there are four or five people, or an entire department in a bank, to deal with these things, the realities and pace of everyday life and business processes frequently still override the theory. In terms of secrets, the situation becomes even more difficult because as the confidential content of information changes over time, so does the access that needs to be given to different people and different things. Thus the situation can in fact change "by itself," yet most companies at the moment are not even geared up to maintain the status quo.

I am certain that there are several thousand users banging their fists on the table or on their keyboard just now, or who feel like throwing their tablet against the wall because they can't access a service they paid for, or which they need for their work, because the system won't let them in. I'm afraid I have bad news for these people as the problem could reach such a degree that a rights matrix will no longer be a case of "may access" or "may not access," but of who can access what exactly and when. Moreover, it's not enough for us to say who has access to what just now, we also need to keep track of who had access yesterday to the same thing. Because when the proverbial stuff hits the fan, we need to know whether six months ago the individual was authorized to access something based on their position, their projects or their assigned tasks back then. And of course, this all needs to be fully in line with the legal regulations (e.g. data protection and data management). Not exactly elegant. Managers are always trained to keep bad news brief. So I'll keep this short: we cannot solve access problems properly.

The thing is that people no longer have a grasp of the whole issue, not even experts all the time, and it is very difficult to find a solution that meets all the conditions. All modern IT systems have some form of rights management, every one guarantees some type of data protection, but how these rights are managed, who can access what and when, and how this is conveyed to the people who constantly work with data-hungry processes and always want to have access to their own data – well, this is no longer easy, in fact, it borders on the impossible.

In addition, unauthorized access often does not involve breaching rules but rather complying with them. Between 2014 and 2016, in successful attacks against banking systems (for example the hack against Bangladesh Bank that caused $81 million of damage, or the hacks against 30 countries in the world causing roughly $900 million of damage), the hackers used targeted mails and sophisticated spyware programs to infiltrate the everyday working activities of the personnel operating banking systems, they mapped and observed them, and by using the data, passwords, and working methods of the staff they then proceeded to carry out transactions that seemed perfectly authentic. So there was not even a hint of circumventing authorization systems or violating processes, everything went fine "on paper." During the OPM scandal that reared its head in the US in 2015-2016, when the personal data of more than 20 million US government staff was stolen, no rights were violated either, in principle they were used properly. So, generally speaking, we can say that once a hacker is "intra domum," or in the house, the security systems do not necessarily see they are there. This is shown by the data, often mentioned in the cybersecurity profession, that hackers, on average, spend 200 days a year residing unnoticed in hacked systems.

And we have not yet touched upon smaller organizations and individuals, where rights management systems virtually do not exist; instead there are passwords and usernames providing fuller access and offering a much weaker and narrower scope of security than large rights management systems. This means that current rights management solutions are difficult to apply effectively in limiting access to secrets, to constantly changing information.

With regard to the email scandal surrounding Hillary Clinton, if former US President Bill Clinton can say in defense of his wife that government organizations and secret service agencies in 2016 have a different understanding of "encrypted" content, and that the whole thing is "so complicated it is difficult to explain to people," then I believe we need to think about the role of machines again. It is possible that this, just like most problems we find difficult, will also be solved by automated technology. Because, after a while, a more intelligent system will probably start to understand what it is currently dealing with, clinical data for example, and that there are three things in it that appear suspicious, so it needs to be forwarded to a physician with an appropriate level of authorization. Don't misunderstand me, these will not be the behavioral systems of today, but will instead be more like artificial intelligence and genuine self-learning programs. We can expect to see solutions that will quickly decide, based on the given situation, who can access certain data and who can't, while also complying with the law. So from now on we can say that machines will only tell people there is a problem or there is something to do when the time comes, and this information will only be shared with those that do not represent a greater risk than is absolutely necessary.

Today however, people can only solve such a problem with limited success, because it is so complicated and intricate that we cannot expect too much of them; what is more, our current data and information protection models ignore secrets and related parameters, which means they are not well suited to automatically determining genuine rights in order to entail the lowest risk possible.

In systems where production takes places solely in the IT sphere (e.g. in financial institutions), the situation is somewhat better. We can say, for example, that cashiers can access the data of account holders, but cannot access all of the bank's budget information, because they don't need to. Bank managers on the other hand can access aggregate daily income or account turnover information, but cannot access the account data of individual clients, because they don't need to.

The issue of rights is very difficult to resolve in situations like healthcare. A huge amount of different data is created here, and it doesn't work only in IT systems, but in environments that differ markedly from one another. These have both a physical and a logical aspect, there is an IT element, a logistics element, and a huge human factor as well (since the "product," people's health, is not a thing either). If some law (e.g. data protection) or IT system places an obstacle in front of, say, a surgical operation or life-saving treatment, this can not only make things difficult sometimes, but even impossible. This results in a situation that is unacceptable for the physicians who have sworn oaths to save lives, for the management responsible for financing the institutions, and for society as a whole. Yet it is still happening with increasing regularity. In February 2016 for example, a heart operation came under threat in a US hospital. The operation had to be suspended for minutes while critical diagnostic equipment used by the physicians was hampered by a slow process traced back to anti-virus software. But limiting access can also cause headaches. For example, a hospital located in the capital of a European country regularly had problems over many years due to strict European data protection laws, because if they stored patients' case-histories in the prescribed manner (i.e. making sure that no unauthorized access was possible), then the attending physicians also experienced problems in accessing the information.

Most organizations have no responsibility to keep themselves safe and secure. They just have to do their thing. But they need to do it securely. And as we descend the size-ladder of companies and organizations, it becomes ever more complicated and troublesome to ensure the right level of protection. Law firms are a good example here, as they tend to work with a negligible number of staff when compared to a production company or a financial institution, while the documents they handle tend to be more important and more sensitive. The Panama offshore scandal that erupted during 2016 centered around a law office that had severely neglected IT security. It is assumed that the hackers stole the 2.6 terabytes of data from the office well beforehand. It has also been alleged that the data had been leaked. Regardless of which version of events is true, it is clear that the lawyers were rather weak with rights and managing unauthorized access. Journalists at the Süddeutsche Zeitung in Germany spent a whole year processing the almost 5 million emails, the more than 2 million PDF files and the several million pieces of other information before publishing the results, and even then they were unable to map out all the inherent links and connections. It is precisely this multi-dimensional content and authorization complexity that presents the real challenge for protection.

Yet in the middle of this rights management and data protection there is a person, an employee, sitting in a law office or the development department of a factory or perhaps in a government office and trying to do his job, just like his employer. His responsibility is limited, but it follows from the above that he can have real influence because we can assume that IT security does not always work on his side. His secrets are at risk, but he's perhaps not aware of this.

But let's imagine a higher-level manager. He is more conscious of the power vested in him and the secrets to be kept because he sees more of the correlations, and the information in his hands is more valuable. Assume he is walking down the street and speaking on the phone to somebody, or wants to tell his wife a story from the office. He needs to think twice about what he should say. He needs to be careful about what he says in public places. The pressure is even greater when he writes an email, replies to a message or shares something on Facebook. The IT risks relating to these secrets can cut the ground from under his feet or from under his company in seconds. A 2016 report by Verizon on security incidents identifies a clear trend underlying the reasons for individual leaks and incidents. Devices of users, and the users themselves, are more responsible for causing these problems than the servers where the data is stored, at a rate increasing by 5% each year: in six years this growth has virtually doubled.

Concerns from more security-conscious managers regarding the risks surrounding organizational secrets often mean that they only dare speak in euphuistic and turgid sentences, using flowery language, both in electronic or telephone communication. And this clearly affects our personal conversations, our private correspondence, and our lives on social media – we are scared, and so we express ourselves more formally. The problems of the human factor transcend far beyond IT, and IT professionals really don't know where to start. We need to consider these problems alongside hacker motivation, complex IT systems, the massive amounts of our data, and the weaknesses of security solutions discussed earlier, in order to look beyond the difficulties and realize that from this angle, rights matrices seem ridiculously simplistic.

It is difficult for a cybersecurity expert to say this, but I feel we are fighting a futile battle against cyber threats, and against ourselves, because we have no idea whether we even have any secrets in today's modern digital world. And if we do, how can we judge that they are secrets? Let's take a look at why this is important.

CHAPTER 7

THE PATH OF SECRETS: ASSESSING MODEL AND RISK

Religion or family? Who will find out?
Is my partner going to leave me?
Unpleasant or problematic secrets.

Whrat is a secret anyway? By definition, a secret is information we don't want others to find out about. "Others" here refers to a person or a group of people (at least for now) as underpinned by our qualitative research on secrets: "A secret is something we deliberately hide from certain people." If our secret has been revealed, the consequences will have a powerful impact on us. If there is fear connected to our secrets, this fear will grow or even become permanent, which can be quite unpleasant.

When this constant state of fear reaches a certain level, we will start to feel anxious and agitated.

A teenage girl in Eastern Europe realizes that she is a lesbian, for instance. She doesn't dare let her family in on this as she is terrified of their reaction. In our modern world digital evidence such as an exchange of emails about visiting a gay bar, or a photo circulated in the social media, is highly likely to be around. Such digital evidence could reveal her secret. She will be increasingly anxious and her concern will be amplified particularly in an online environment where there are vast amounts of data which private individuals cannot control, carrying the ever-increasing risk of connections being made from the various interlinked sets of information and the secret being revealed.

There are things we know we should hide, and there are things where we just aren't sure. Or we aren't sure which part of the secret we should be hiding — so we choose to hide all of it. And as to how well we should hide it (who may know about it, how long it should remain a secret; which respected set of norms are we violating with the secret? and does it jeopardize our existence?) varies from secret to secret. Consequently, we often have to re-assess our secrets, and we do so in ourselves, but this almost never translates into doing something about the security of our data and information behind our secrets in cyberspace. In short: we generally do not re-classify our secrets on the internet or on our computers just because their environment or our attitude towards those secrets has changed. Companies, public administration, law enforcement authorities, and secret service agencies do re-classify their secrets or their level of confidentiality, but much more slowly than changes occur at the true level, the changing value or risk of the secret.

A lot of other things can happen to secrets. We can create them, manage them, find out about them — they can get leaked. Or we can be happy about them: no one knows other than ourselves.

Whatever happens to our secrets, whether they're created, obtained, kept or uncovered, this can affect our emotions. Whether it makes us sad or nervous depends on the type of the secret — but we can be glad if, for instance, we can protect the more intimate secrets of our relationships. Let me share a personal experience with you: A couple were preparing to celebrate their wedding anniversary on a cruise trip, and their children wanted to prepare a surprise for them. At the end of the trip the couple's favorite song was played from the loudspeakers of the ship, the very song that was played at their wedding. The couple couldn't believe it. "But how did you find out? We never told you!" They were truly happy about the wonderful and formerly well-kept secret, even now that it has been revealed. But finding out, for example, about the solutions proposed by your rivals when placing an offer, will give you strategic information and a competitive edge.

You need to know what can be uncovered or not, where the simple obtaining and keeping of that secret is a secret per se. It's really sad if a dear friend finds out far too soon what surprise they are getting for their birthday. It's awkward when you are talking to someone with your back to the door and the moment you turn around you find that the last sentence of the conservation has been overheard by someone who shouldn't have. It's equally embarrassing when a recipient is somehow added to an exchange of emails, someone who should not be part of it. In that moment it's hard to know how you should feel about it. Should I be ashamed or not? Should I offer an explanation? And how should I go about the whole thing anyway?

We can apply this to companies and organizations too, who feel just the same. When the data of a bank's clients is threatened or when a security company gets broken into, the same principle is observable, only raised to another level.

When Gamma, a company developing spyware for governments, was hacked in the summer of 2014, some 40 gigabytes of stolen data was revealed to the whole world within hours. The data showed exactly how their government spyware application FinFisher worked, which countries had already purchased the product and how much they had spent on it; the leaked emails even highlighted installation and operation problems. What can the government of a democratic country tell its people to explain that they have spent so much taxpayers' money on the surveillance of as many people as possible, and that things have, unfortunately, not worked out as they hoped, because they were either unable to use the program or they bought the wrong product. An equally interesting question is what a security company should do when it gets hacked, and the secrets of their confidential governmental clients are revealed.

As I said before, when it comes to analyzing risks there is an impact assessment method to determine what kinds of risk can potentially threaten a system, data or a piece of information, the probability of this risk, and its potential impact if the problem does occur. The results will give us a good idea of what we need to protect. At least in theory. Given the losses of over $400 million pocketed annually by cybercriminals, stolen personal data in the tens of millions and gigabytes of corporate, and government emails leaked, it's safe to say that this protection is not very effective in practice. Not very effective because it fails to focus on the right secret to be protected.

When we specify the level of a secret to ourselves, the very essence of that secret is filtered through an entire process which will, eventually, tell us how at risk we consider our various secrets to be. Information and data are fundamentally different from secrets in that a secret builds a context around itself and demands continual examination of the context in which we can interpret the given information. A secret doesn't make any sense without knowing who can find out about it. This fundamentally affects what we think about it, how valuable it is to us, and what we are ready to do to prevent a person or people from finding it out. For example, the fact you lost your job badge weeks ago and you have been "sneaking in" ever since must be hidden from the security guys at your company: which is the most important goal when protecting this secret.

Other elements of the context can also be essential, such as the timeframe, another key element of secrets. The secret, for example, that you found out from an email that accidentally landed in your inbox, that a major market-leading manufacturer listed on the stock exchange will acquire another company, is a secret worth a fortune today, but will not be one tomorrow; only five people know about it today but tomorrow the whole world will know.

"Where?" is another vital question. Suppose that the processing plant of a UK company producing meat products, mainly for Indian export, receives a pork delivery, which is duly processed and the finished products are transported to the country of destination. A colleague at logistics spots a few weeks later that that the copy of the delivery note he received in an email, says that the actual content of the original consignment was beef, and the management knew about this. Revealing such a secret really matters in India, where it is strictly forbidden by religious requirements to eat the meat of cows, which are considered sacred. If this secret came to light, it would have a clear and direct impact on sales in that particular area.

But it's not necessarily the context that we examine first. Sometimes we classify our secret based on more than one norm, and we assess this first. Such norms are, say, social expectations or religious rules, but also laws. Suppose that in your own religious and cultural environment it is most inappropriate and therefore forbidden to enter a place of worship half naked, then you will try to hide from everybody that three years ago you popped in a church on your way home to cool off in that scorching heat, without your shirt on. It could be particularly embarrassing if, driven by guilt, you confessed this on Facebook to your best friend who is not your best friend anymore. Your neighbor may even have a video of the whole thing on her smartphone.

Your place of work or business life can have a similar effect in setting norms. Your secret might violate some business ethic, or a job regulation, operating or compliance policy. In 2016 some two billion mistakenly addressed emails or mistakenly attached documents caused severe problems around the globe. When, for example, a distributor sends his price list to a retailer, also including the columns showing his own disproportionately high profits. Or when the contracting entity's office accidentally sends one of the bidders the sheet containing the prices by all of the other rival bidders. Such secrets cannot be "undone," even if the people involved in the situation try to behave in a fair way. So square one in the case of such secrets is adhering to the norms when we assess the risks carried by a given secret.

When assessing their secret, individuals may look at it with an eye to the risk it poses for their own needs. For human and corporate needs we have a rather good model, Maslow's categories, which distinguishes our basic and our higher needs. Psychologist Abraham Maslow defined these needs as a pyramid containing a hierarchy of layers, where the most fundamental physical needs such as eating are at the bottom and the need for self-actualization at the top. The model has been widely praised and criticized in equal measure, but we have yet to come up with a more workable theory. When we assess a secret from the point of view of the threat it poses to our needs, we do not necessarily have to stick to the structure of this pyramid. It suffices to accept the various categories and that individuals do differentiate between fundamental needs (such as home, food, and belongings) and higher levels.

For example, a CEO reads an email flow addressed to him and notices that in an email forwarded earlier on, his confidant and a key expert at the company makes nasty comments about him and the company itself. Now he must seriously consider whether to keep the secret he has discovered to himself, and if so, how. Revealing the secret would jeopardize one of the most important layers of basic corporate needs, because dismissing or disciplining the person could endanger the operation of the organization. Keeping the secret could be a source of many problems in the future, so revealing it carries a great risk. Also, the employee should have been more careful with his secret, he should have known that if it comes out it would badly tarnish his reputation and might even harm his livelihood: so if it's revealed, it could affect his fundamental needs.

Thus when assessing a secret, we consider three aspects:

1. Assessing the context – e.g. who, when, and where.
2. Assessing the norm – e.g. laws, cultural, and religious customs.
3. Assessing our needs – e.g. food, love, and self-actualization. We do not consider the various aspects independently of each

other but relying on one another, we actually walk around. There is always a point of entry into this assessment circle. Suppose we decide that the problem is that a particular person has found out about our secret, in which case we entered the assessment circle at the point of the context. Suppose our secret violates a family tradition (e.g. you want to marry someone from another village) then the point of entry was your norms. Our needs can also serve as points of entry in the assessment circle. After this, however, we "visit" all of the points in our minds and make an assessment. The individual aspects of assessment do have an impact on one another.

Finally, the result of the process, an assessment or feeling about the factors threatening our secret "gets fed into" a coordinate system-like space, where we decide what to make of the given secret, personally or from an organizational point of view; we determine how awkward, (embarrassing or even tragic) or how problematic its consequences might be, which could in turn cause even greater difficulty for us. For the 50-year old man that I am, it is embarrassing but not problematic if I like sleeping with pink stuffed toys, for example. It's problematic but not embarrassing if I keep hiding the mail from a malicious resident "at war" with the others in my apartment block.

Under the heading of embarrassing or tragic consequences, most of the time we keep secrets whose revelation to others of our own accord would affect our intimacy with that person, since the secret is about something we only share with people really close to us. When it comes to our relationship to a secret from an organization's point of view, we step into the organization's shoes and this is how our attitude to the secret is defined.

Secrets relating to typically problematic areas are usually linked to severe violations of norms. Violating laws, regulations, and rules: all of them can have direct, major or far-reaching consequences.

There are secrets that can be both unpleasant and problematic at the same time, such as the Volkswagen emissions scandal that erupted in September 2015. It was revealed that the company falsified emissions data by modifying the software of its cars to show better emissions results in tests. This is not only illegal (conflicting with laws) and amounts to a huge loss based on one of the largest damages ever awarded (altogether more than $25 billion) which affects the basic needs of the organization, but it also badly tarnished the company's reputation. The disclosure of this secret was not only embarrassing but also deeply problematic for the company.

When we find the point in the coordination system above that best fits our personal relationship to the secret, then we have reached the end of the process. This process takes place in our minds for each and every secret, sometimes longer or shorter, slower or faster. When it occurs to us to question whether we can send a particular company email, whether we can share something on Twitter, whether we can post a particular picture on Instagram or whether we can download a given document; we consider who would see it, whether the disclosure would conform to norms, which of our needs it would affect, and whether it would be embarrassing or if we could even get ourselves in trouble in the end. The specific information we want to disclose does not contain the secret itself, it creates it at the end of the assessment process.

99% of all IT system users copy data, upload information, fill in forms, and write emails, and do not handle secrets. This is exactly why they do not know what to make of the security classification of data, they have a hard time telling what they should do with certain pieces of information, whether they can be put down in writing, to whom, and in how much detail. There are rules, expectations, and recommendations but most of the time we go for it on a gut feeling, which is based on our assessment and classification of that personal secret. This means we tear up the rule book of logic and of the IT security risk analysis explained earlier, in our daily or organizational lives we make decisions about the secret value of a given piece of information or a context along the lines of the above assessment, disregarding instructions like "strictly confidential." The remaining 1%, people who work with secrets and confidential information as their profession, may not make decisions as required by the rules either, but they tend to give more weight to these rules when analyzing the normative environment of a secret. They take a good look at what the rules, the law, and the organizational expectations require, and think twice before violating these norms, but in their own minds they assess the personal risk of the secret coming out all the same.

The coordinate system of personal or organizational attitudes can be divided into three large groups. These categories are called white, gray, and black secrets. Secrets that are unpleasant (e.g. embarrassing) when they are revealed but will not cause a major problem are white secrets. Black secrets can be criminal acts (say, tax fraud or domestic violence) that will definitely tarnish the person's reputation if revealed and can cause a major problem (e.g. imprisonment, criminal record). Gray secrets are somewhere in between and their assessment wavers between black and white. They can be less problematic; white secrets in a more accommodating and open world, and black secrets in certain norm environments (due to religious rules, for example). A white secret is the light version, something we do not advertise and something that could be rather unpleasant if others find out about it, so it is something to worry about. A black secret tends to be something we are ashamed about.

In the table below you can find a few examples illustrating the classification of secrets. Obviously, the normative environment, your needs, and the context can all affect these classifications. There are countries where not paying your taxes for two years is not only illegal but also unpleasant. Among young urban atheists, sacrilege in a church will probably count as a white secret, and only problematic.

Suppose you live in religious Middle-Eastern country, then peeping on your friend's wife would be a problematic black secret instead of a gray one.

Personal evaluation	White Secret	Grey Secret	Black Secret
Tendency to be unpleasant Embarrassing / tragic consequences	I always sleep in the very same pair of blue socks	I washed my hands in the church with holy water	I blackmailed my ex with his/her naked pictures
Tendency to be a problem Could end up in trouble	I'm sick but I won't see a doctor	I spied on my friend's wife while she was having a bath	I haven't paid my taxes for two years

The figure below shows the risk analysis process of a secret, which produces the risk level of the secret.

Process of risk evaluation for secrets

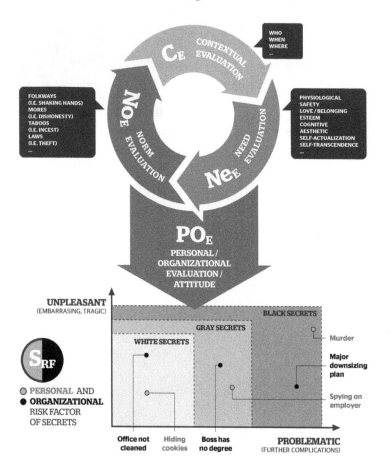

WHO
WHEN
WHERE
...

C_E CONTEXTUAL EVALUATION

No_E NORM EVALUATION

Ne_E NEED EVALUATION

FOLKWAYS
(I.E. SHAKING HANDS)
MORES
(I.E. DISHONESTY)
TABOOS
(I.E. INCEST)
LAWS
(I.E. THEFT)
...

PHYSIOLOGICAL
SAFETY
LOVE / BELONGING
ESTEEM
COGNITIVE
AESTHETIC
SELF-ACTUALIZATION
SELF-TRANSCENDENCE
...

PO_E
PERSONAL /
ORGANIZATIONAL
EVALUATION /
ATTITUDE

UNPLEASANT
(EMBARRASING, TRAGIC)

BLACK SECRETS

GRAY SECRETS

WHITE SECRETS

Murder

Major
downsizing
plan

Spying on
employer

S_RF

● PERSONAL AND
● ORGANIZATIONAL
RISK FACTOR
OF SECRETS

Office not
cleaned

Hiding
cookies

Boss has
no degree

PROBLEMATIC
(FURTHER COMPLICATIONS)

CHAPTER 8

IN THE LAND OF SECRETS: ESSENCE AND EXPOSURE

"I can explain..."

If we decide that our secret is at risk, and its protection is inefficient or non-existent, then we seek alternative solutions. For example, we can add a new rule to ignorance, negligence or prayers: don't get caught! Getting caught is equal to the disclosure of the secret, and it can be easier to deal with than protecting the secret. You often hear people say, "I'll explain if it comes out." This is actually a rather characteristic and frequently employed way of handling risks, and surprisingly enough, large organizations apply it instinctively.

So what should we do if our secret has been revealed? Denial is a tried and tested strategy; for instance, Lauri Love, a 31-year-old IT expert from the UK, denies having hacked the computers of NASA and the US Federal Reserve, and won't reveal the passwords encoding his devices. At least for now, these passwords are preventing his extradition to the US.

Another way of tackling this is to leak secrets that divert attention from the truly important ones. During the 2016 US presidential election campaign, for example, a security company was requested to investigate the IT system of the Democratic National Commission. They did so of course at the request of the owner, i.e. ethically. They found that the DNC's system had been broken into by Russian hackers more than a year earlier and had suffered data theft. Two hacker groups were identified, operating under the names of Cozy Bear and Fancy Bear, which security experts refer to under the codenames of APT 28 and APT 29. The former has been carrying out actions against key targets such as air traffic, defense, energy sector or government systems since the mid-2000s, and can probably be linked to Russian intelligence. They likely made this public because their customer, the DNC, allowed them to do so. In all likelihood they knew all too well that the hackers had accessed documents that could cause political turmoil if leaked, particularly towards the end of the 2016 presidential election campaign, and it seemed better to preempt this. So they went for the "Russian scenario," which could even be true of course, and accused the two hacker groups of the hack. But then all of a sudden a lone hacker turns up calling himself Guccifer 2.0, purporting to be of Romanian origin. He claimed to have carried out the hacks and found it particularly flattering that Crowdstrike, conducting the investigation, thought so highly of his skills that they imagined several Russian hacker groups to have been necessary for such complex attacks. He even claims to have accessed the systems of the DNC using surprisingly simple methods, without any complicated hocus pocus, so that neither the intricate attack technique nor the Russian hacker groups are real, he says. To demonstrate that he does indeed possess the political documents stolen from the DNC, he published a few pages, including detailed analyses on the Republican candidate, Donald Trump, as well as national security reports and documents from Hillary Clinton's time as a member of the Administration. He also said that he had handed them over alongside other information to Wikileaks, which specializes in publishing leaked documents; and that Wikileaks would soon disclose them. In the meantime, however, the hacker remained active himself, publishing morsels from the DNC's box of secrets now and then.

So the following question arises: who has actually been into the DNC servers? However obvious it may seem that a security company should know the answer, in fact they do not. They can draw conclusions and they have indeed done so, as confirmed by other experts and companies. But can someone not say this for sure? If you want to understand the situation a cyber detective is in when trying to nail the answer to a question like that, then imagine finding traces left behind by insects in your house. You call an exterminator and give them the following wish list:

1. Tell me what insects entered my house
2. Categorize them by insect groups
3. Find their nest (if there is one) and eliminate them
4. Tell me when they entered the house

5. How long they stayed

6. How often they entered

7. What food they accessed

8. And how many morsels they took from the pantry

9. Tell me why they came

10. What they could potentially do with the food they took

11. And can you please provide evidence for all the above...

If you have never asked an exterminator to do all this, you really should. After a few moments of light-hearted amusement together, you'll be told that this borders on the impossible.

In contrast to the example above, there is an additional difficulty in cybersecurity: data does not tend to disappear or become moth-eaten. It is simply copied and the copies are taken by the thieves, so that it is really impossible to tell exactly what they have taken, at most you can establish what they accessed.

This is because most organizations do not properly log, record, and store information on what data was accessed by whom and when, particularly if the attackers did not obtain the data in the usual, official route. This is why it is difficult or downright impossible later on to tell which data is affected if there has been a data theft.

So it is only natural that publishing disinformation, half-true information or information believed to be half true, can provide a workable solution for cases when you get busted. Furthermore, as the examples above amply illustrate, this can be used effectively by both parties (the attacker and the victim).

But the situation can escalate. Sometimes you cannot escape the inevitable, the secret will get out. In the pre-digital world, supporting or conclusive evidence for secrets was few and far between. You could explain away just about anything, or deny it verbally.

In ancient Egyptian law, agreements were concluded verbally up until the 7th century BC, and cases in medieval Europe were decided after trying to entangle often contradictory statements, with eye- and ear-witnesses, the power of the spoken word, playing a decisive role. In the course of history, the degree to which written documents supported the truth of spoken words varied from time to time, but law and society have always treated evidence in a different way. The US legal system knows the notion of hearsay evidence: statements like, "I was told this or that was heard," which is inadmissible as evidence in court, is very much admissible in society. In human relationships it is even common that we would prefer to believe a reference person we know (a parent, a friend or a celebrity) rather than a written document.

The appearance of photographs in the first half of the 19th century, and their widespread use in the late 1800s, led to a reevaluation of the weight of oral evidence and oral statements. Photographs contained something stronger than words, an image we could see for ourselves. Although the supporters of evolutionary biology disagree on whether seeing or hearing "came first" in ontogeny, many of us still hold that "seeing is believing." People retouching photographs used this effect to their advantage (a trend we see to this day) and started to manipulate photographs to produce false evidence of the truth, thus influencing opinions. It is no coincidence that the photo retouching machinery supported by the censors of the Party leadership of the Soviet Union worked for decades from the 1920s with remarkable efficiency. Following orders, members of the propaganda organization frequently removed "anti-system elements" and "enemies of the Party" from group or personal photos. In this way they practically eliminated evidence even to the extent of a person having ever existed. Books evidencing ideological secrets shared the same fate, in Moscow alone millions of books were destroyed annually in the 1930s.

Even so, it is a fact that the arrival of the digital age and the appearance of digital photography with smart devices has provided new opportunities to get busted via an image. Just remember the amateur videos of the police using excessive force in the US that were circulated in the summer of 2016, which resulted in political demonstrations and further victims.

So are our secrets bound to be revealed and proven? No, far from it. Confidence in digital images and videos is not strong enough yet, as devices suitable for manipulating data even in your home are readily available, the professional use of which will give you stunningly deceptive results. Photoshopping is an ever-present issue when evaluating fashion shots or pictures shared in social media, but the amateur editing of videos has also improved greatly over the last decade or so. Zach King, for instance, in his popular amateur videos, records himself in his daily routine via his smartphone, when all of a sudden he will do something that seems physically impossible, or some seemingly impossible things will happen to him. For example trimming a Christmas tree in one fluid motion, or an incredible jump into a fast-moving car through the window. We get the feeling that this ordinary guy possess magical powers. So what's the case then with digital evidence? Do we believe it or not? Funnily enough, we cannot rid ourselves of our evolutionary heritage despite all these trick photos, and manipulated or misleading information. What we can see or hear is stronger than what we want to know or believe. Impulses targeting our ears and eyes even throw down the gauntlet with seemingly contradictory facts.

A perfect example of this is the key role Excel spreadsheets play in corporate business flows, their high position in the corporate ecosystem of beliefs, if you will. Almost any data we enter into an Excel spreadsheet appreciates in value and we are more willing to believe it simply because it takes the form of figures in a neatly organized environment. This belief can linger on even after we have confirmed that the data is incorrect. The reference environment, its form, and the structure, simply deceives our senses, while we often want to believe, and this credulity itself plays a role. So I would suggest that if you are uncertain about your ability to persuade, you should use Excel, it's excellent therapy and promises great results.

The source of the information is another question. As I mentioned before, we are more willing to believe a reference person.

This also goes for sources of news, websites, and other sources of data that we consider to be reliable (e.g. radio, television, podcast, feeds, etc). When assessing the content of information we also consider its source, which raises yet another question concerning the authenticity of digital sources of information: is what we believe to be authentic really authentic? If hackers can break into your private mailbox and steal personalities, why couldn't they do the same with a source of data? Unfortunately, not only can they do this, but they already do. The Al Jazeera news broadcaster has been attacked a number of times, including one instance when the hackers broke into their newsletter service and published false news about the death of Sheikh Hamad bin Jassem, then Prime Minister of Qatar. A similar attack was directed against the French television channel TV5Monde in 2015, which was thought at first to have been committed by the cyber army of ISIS, the "Cyber Caliphate," but later on the hacker group known as APT28, with links to Russia (and probably involved in the attack against the DNC) came under the spotlight. Attacks like these are carried out for propaganda purposes or to cause disruptions, and there can also be underlying economic reasons behind them. This is why global news sources are not the only potential targets of attacks like these. Websites, Twitter or Facebook accounts of public figures, celebrities, and well-known businessmen are broken into on a regular basis. Remember the "roadshow" of the hacktivist team OurMine in the summer of 2016? When the various social media pages of Facebook boss Mark Zuckenberg, Twitter CEO Jack Dorsey, the inventor of Pokemon GO John Hanke, and many other well-known public figures, were hacked one after another to post messages on them?

If our secrets are revealed, there can be visual or written evidence against us that supports the authenticity and reliability of the disclosed information. At the same time, however, a lot depends on what sources the evidence comes from, in what environment, format, and structure they are available, and also on which of our senses we choose to believe. On the other side of the equation, we encounter the uncertainty which affects our evaluation of the authenticity of the data available digitally today, particularly from the Internet. This pushes us towards a digital data confidence problem, which could easily evolve into a crisis, given that our modern economic and human systems depend crucially on IT solutions and on the accessibility, availability, integrity, and authenticity of the data in them. This is exactly what we trust less and less.

When a secret is revealed you cannot make a precise estimate of the consequences. It may not even be newsworthy if only one element of the puzzle is leaked. But if someone matches it with another element, maybe from another source, then the secret put together in this way may result in a much bigger problem. In 2015, the Indian security researcher Sathya Prakash identified a security vulnerability in the mobile application of an unnamed bank, which he claimed to be severe enough that it could lead to money being stolen from any of the bank's clients. It was later confirmed that using this method, up to $25 billion could have been stolen from the largest bank in India. In early 2016 the SWIFT scandal erupted when hackers stole $81 million from Bangladesh Bank, and similar cases came to light one after the other in the following months. The actual connection between these cases is immaterial: tiny bits of secrets were eventually forged into newsworthy items made known to, and digestible for, the general public.

CHAPTER 9

DOWN THE WELL OF SECRETS: VALUES AND DILEMMAS

*The stock exchange of secrets,
the secrecy-switch, and systems
that see everything*

Just like the status of a secret, its quality is not unique either. This gives us a distinct opportunity to experiment on the author. My white secret, for instance, that I swapped a Modern Talking poster with a schoolmate in primary school for an old Playboy magazine, is a secret of variable quality. Why? Because you do not yet know whether I gave or was given the poster.

But it can be a real scandal if it comes out that a bank's CEO goes to a swinger club or takes heroin. If, however, the passwords of thousands or millions of clients are made public, that's a very different cup of tea. Or suppose that the heroin habit of the bank CEO is less interesting for the public, but all the more so for a hacker group. Blackmailing the CEO, they gain money or indirect financial advantages. Or they can get completely different kinds of information from him and the original secret will not be leaked. One of the corporate risks most difficult to detect and therefore one of the most dreaded, by the way, is the blackmailing of staff or top executives. In these situations the secret will not actually become public, illustrating the fact that the status of a secret, or its life cycle, does not necessarily have only two states, in terms of whether it exists or not, or whether it is revealed or not. It could also be "in motion." When LinkedIn and other major systems were broken into in 2011-2012, the hundreds of millions of username/password pairs taken by various hacker groups for subsequent break-ins were probably used successfully, as the databases were not made public and they were not put up for sale on the black market either. Some of them perhaps remained secret for a small group, but the fact of their existence was revealed, and for the victims attacked by the hackers, whose data was used in this way, the secrets ceased to be secrets. A few years later, however, probably due to an internal conflict among the hackers, a lot of the data appeared for sale on the dark web, for a few dollars per password. The secrets had been reclassified and as a result, in mid-2016, the information was used to hack the accounts of tech CEOs like Mark Zuckerberg and led to the leak of Dropbox's 68 million user accounts from the 2012 hack.

Sometimes blackmailing does not bring visible results and the change in the status of the secret does not have much of an impact. In 2016 there were several incidents where hackers entered the internal IT system of an organization to take their data, then blackmailed the company for money, threatening to publish the sensitive data. In April 2016, hackers stole a vast amount of personal data, payroll lists, and other sensitive information, amounting to 14.8 gigabytes, from the Canadian gold mining company Goldcorp. This was used to blackmail the mining company and some of the stolen data was actually published. Goldcorp's CEO said he was not afraid of anything embarrassing coming to light as the company had always operated publicly. Remember what Gartner predicted would occur by 2020? We will make publicly accessible that which we are unable to protect, and we will try to protect the rest much more carefully.

But if the status and the value of a secret are constantly changing, does that make secrets a form of commodity or share? As you can see, the data at the heart of the secret can be sold and bought, it can be located in several places at the same time and can even be multiplied; but as long as it stays within a confidential circle, and as long as the status of the secret remains unchanged, the value of the secret will not change either. We should probably regard secrets as shares, the value of which depends mostly on its status, e.g. public or not public, whether it has been revealed or not, or how many people know about it.

In the UK an investigation into the rape of a female student was closed, or to be precise, put on the back burner by the police. They decided they could not proceed with the case. Then the hacker group Anonymous published a video providing fresh evidence as well as the identity of the man that they suspected to be the rapist. They published his phone number, his email address, and everything the hackers believed to be important, so that the police were forced to relaunch the case. Anonymous justified their actions, saying that they wanted to encourage the police to do their job and investigate. This means that the secret had probably been in the hands of Anonymous all along, and until it became public it was not that interesting, but the moment it did become public, the significance of the secret soared. That said, Anonymous could have used this secret for other purposes, they could have started to make the man's life hell, as they knew so many things about him, or they could have served justice, which is not uncommon for a hacktivist group, Anonymous being no exception. It is also possible that if the police had done nothing after this action, then they would have "taken revenge." So this specific secret, containing the personal data of the man, was one with a variable life cycle, status, and value. At this point it is actually worthless as it has become public.

Peter Swire, a member of the team briefing President Obama in intelligence and communication issues (such as in the private sphere vs security dilemma) shares the view that the life cycle of secrets is constantly shrinking. For Swire, secrets that in the past would have been kept for 25 years, come out much sooner than that nowadays. In addition to the insecurity typical of cyberspace and the multi-faceted motivation of threat factors, this is also due to the social phenomenon of decreasing faculties: people have an increasingly shorter attention and concentration span. A Microsoft survey in 2015 suggests that the average attention span, the length of time we can concentrate on something, has reduced from 12 to 8 seconds since the appearance of mobile internet devices (around the year 2000). This represents a 33% drop in 15 years. If it continues to change at this pace, we'll be losing one second every year. By 2020 our attention might be sustainable for an average period of 6-7 seconds only. Everything is accelerating. I keep telling people waiting for elevators, who are complaining about its speed, that I don't think there is anything wrong with the elevator, it is we who have accelerated. Given this speed and other technical factors, it is no wonder that the life cycle of secrets is also getting shorter.

Cybersecurity experts have been toying with the idea for quite a while now that something should be done about the problem of users who find it tough to handle the security settings and safe operation of their software and smart devices. But unfortunately they have no brilliant ideas that could do the trick, so they don't exactly push the issue. Yet Bruce Schneier, a renowned cryptographer and cybersecurity expert in the US, does have an idea. At the Hacktivity Conference in Hungary in 2010, he said that the security sector should come up with foolproof solutions, ones that do not give users much to do because they provide adequate safety in themselves. If you think about it, everyday objects surrounding us are already like that: the average car or television is hard to damage by using it. But information technology, today at least, is completely different. A crypto-virus is perfectly capable of breaking our connection to the rest of the world in a few minutes, and it takes about the same time to paralyze the operation of an entire hospital or organization as we saw in 2015 and 2016 in several institutions of healthcare in the US and in Eastern Europe. A virus like this can destroy research results over months or years even, in the product development and research divisions of pharmaceutical companies for example, samples worth tens of thousands of dollars are destroyed every month due to computer virus attacks. Apple recognized soon enough that the majority of its users do not really like fumbling with security settings and do not want to have to learn another profession completely, just to be able to use their computers and phones. Living up to the promise of being easy to handle and use, iPhones and iPads using the iOS operating system made a big splash. It seems straightforward, therefore, that we should be developing "foolproof" systems, which are safe enough as they are, leaving nothing for the user to do. For example, when we have written an email and are about to send it, the body of the message could turn another color, to indicate that we have written something which may not be a good idea to send. These are two ends of the very same algorithm, making usage easy and protecting the user.

A high-end smartphone today can encode its own content in a way that not even its owner knows how it was done. In this way, the phone essentially protects its user from their own stupidity. But this is still far from perfect, as our phone or computer still does not know today what is more or less important information for us, and knows even less about our secrets. Let there be no mistake, we are definitely not talking about whether a browser can tell if we have entered a site with data theft or malicious programs, or if our mailing program spots that we are about to send someone credit card information in a mail. The security industry should put solutions on the table that can learn, interpret things, and act on our behalf, meaning that they can protect the user from their own careless mistakes, just like cars and televisions do. This raises another question, the issue of using artificial intelligence, i.e. thinking computers, in security devices. Elon Musk, founder of Tesla, paints a rather dark picture of the development and use of such solutions, which is hard to ignore. In the summer of 2016, the Cyber Grand Challenge in Las Vegas was organized by DARPA (Defense Advanced Research Projects Agency) which is the military defense research agency of the US Department of Defense, to whom we partly owe our thanks for the Internet, by the way. The goal set at the Challenge was no less than creating automated and self-learning intelligence able to detect vulnerabilities in cybersecurity systems, which Musk regards as the potential origin of the "hostile artificial intelligence" of the future, "Skynet," if you like, from the *Terminator* series. Renowned researcher and theoretical physicist Stephen Hawking says that in 100 years everything will be controlled by machines, probably ones envisioned by DARPA, instead of people, but by that time, given the current conditions of cyberspace, it seems sensible to teach humans how to protect their own secrets. Here I must emphasize the word "secret" rather than data or information; the security sector has already been trying to teach people how to protect the latter two, withoutmuch success.

One fundamental principal is that the more you understand the risks relating to a secret and the risks of that secret being revealed, the better you can protect your secrets, since the risk lies not in data getting stolen or information intercepted, but in the exposure of a secret. This is no easy task even in reality, let alone in digital space. Thinking in terms of risks is an uncomfortable and generally not-so-positive thinking pattern, it's not very pleasant to think about what will happen if the worst-case scenario does actually happen. Because most people don't think in terms of risks, they do not really feel the need to protect themselves. Although the number of situations where you are exposed to circumstances like these is not infinite or impossible to define, it's not the situations you need to learn one by one and it's not the various types of risks you need to explore in depth. What you need to learn and apply is the principle itself. This is the kind of behavior cybersecurity experts call security-awareness, which is even taught, but it is simply the very human practice of avoiding risk-focused thinking that makes it impossible to translate this in practice. It is therefore not a coincidence that the information security awareness training run since the early 2000s by the OPM (Office of Personal Management, the US government agency that manages the personal data of government employees) was ultimately pointless since it could not prevent the presumably Chinese military hackers who took the personal data of the OPM's own employees in 2014 and 2015 to steal the most sensitive personal data of more than 20 million US government employees, stirring up quite a political and personnel scandal.

As a rule, police officers must record the measures they take via cameras in their cars. One such video captured a case where a police officer stopped a motorist on the freeway to identify her. While they were standing in front of the cars, checking the driver's data, the policeman asked the driver twice to move over from the side of her car, away from the freeway, as anything could happen due to the heavy traffic, even though they were standing on the shoulder. The driver ignored the officer's request both times and stayed next to her car. When the officer called a third time, the driver unwillingly walked from her car towards the edge of the freeway, closer to the officer. Three seconds later, a car suddenly left the row of the passing vehicles and crashed into the driver's car at incredible speed, hitting the exact spot where the driver had been standing a few seconds before she did as she was told by the officer. The officer looked up from the papers and said in a perfectly calm voice, "See? That's what I meant."

One of the reasons why security-awareness training is generally doomed to failure is to be found in human nature per se, in our approach to risks, to be precise. There are two fundamental ways to reduce risks. One is to obtain information. Risks will always increase when we are faced with something unknown. If we do not have any information about what is going to happen, we do not understand the situation. Finding ourselves in a situation where we don't have a good understanding and a clear view will make us scared. If we have no information about something, we can reduce the tension this creates by ignoring it. So we typically tend to do one of two things: we either obtain the information we need to reduce our insecurity, or we ignore the situation. In this seemingly convoluted world of cybersecurity, your average person, and I'm sorry to say but also your average business, will generally regard the first as the privilege of experts and tends to do the latter. Meaning they choose not to do deal with the problem. Hiding behind the excuse of "I don't see why this is necessary and it's a hassle anyway," average users at home tend to neglect updating the programs on their phones or computers; a survey by Secunia in 2016 suggested that even today, one in ten users do not update their programs. Another general phenomenon is that people do not change their passwords, which landed millions of users in danger when hundreds of millions of passwords, stolen in hacker activities back in 2011 and 2012, turned up in 2016 on internet black markets. Many of the passwords were still valid even after 4-5 years. Users also believe that settings are too complicated. A study by American university researchers published in 2014 grouped Facebook users into six categories depending on the extent and the way they used their privacy settings. More than one in five ended up in the "minimum user" category, at the same time that the little blue dinosaur appeared in the Facebook sidebar, which was supposed to guide users in the complicated realm of security and private settings.

Businesses, too, have their excuses for ignoring risks. Professor Alastair Beresford, from Cambridge University, says in an article, published in 2016 in the Wall Street Journal, that companies have to decide whether to employ their limited resources to come up with new devices or to fix the security deficiencies of the old ones. Economic motivation enters this question too, as organizations choose to look ahead rather than to mend shortcomings, which is costly and does not incentivize consumers to buy new products.

The good news is that there are still some who do choose to face the challenges of reducing risks. As I have already pointed out, they have three tasks: they have to know what they have, what dangers are lurking around them, and how they can protect what they have.

Risks can be reduced considerably by simply having a clear picture of what information we have of a personal nature, that could pose a risk. Everyone knows, for instance, that they have their health and that this can be at risk. It is also a risk if it is cold outside and yet we refuse to put a hat on. But this is a risk we can manage because we spent our childhood listening to Mom lecturing us to put our hats on. We may have fallen into the trap and thought that not wearing one will make us look cool, but then we caught a cold and had our fair share of all the nasty side effects of a cold. Such risks are easier to understand, we have information about them, about our health and capacity to work. Such risks can be managed as a matter of routine.

There are many more things, however, that we have less information about. The list of valuables required by insurance companies is a good example of this. When we take out an insurance policy, in theory we are supposed to hand over a continuously updated list of our movable property. Many of us get stuck just at this stage: they have no idea as to exactly what they possess. Digging deeper, say, to the level of knives, napkins, and bars of soap, we realize that we have no idea about what we have. The storage capacity of our brain equals roughly 2.5 petabytes of data, hundreds of millions of television shows or videos watched, we remember about 10,000 faces and we recognize around 90% of 3,000 items we have seen before. Still, in the short term we remember four to seven objects or events and when asked what the ten items we popped out to the shops for were, we are unable to recall even half of them.

Nonetheless, these are physical things; even greater chaos seems to prevail when it comes to IT issues. If you ask an average user to list what data he has currently on his laptop, he would have a hard time even naming the larger categories. When prompted to remember the typical categories, e.g. photos? tax returns? bank accounts? they would suddenly realize just how much they actually have. To give you an idea, let's take photos only. Even modest estimates suggest that in 2015 about 1000 to 2000 billion photos (mainly digital images) were taken in a year, which leaves us with more than a thousand new photos on each and every telephone and computer in a year, calculating on the basis of three photos a day. No wonder, therefore, that most people do not know exactly what IT "assets" they have. And it's the same for most businesses, since people work there too, using far more data. In one attack against Sony Pictures, hackers are alleged to have taken

100 terabytes of data, but the information taken in an average hacker attack could also amount to several gigabytes of data. It's only natural that the issue of information assets is highly popular with auditors assessing the security of organizations.

Secrets are made up of the content, links, contexts, and timeframes of data and information assets, and many more factors taken together, creating the secret wealth of companies and private individuals. This is a package, a collection of multi-dimensional secrets made up of complex effects, and we are most vulnerable to it being leaked and revealed.

Thus we already have a fuzzy situation at the first stage of obtaining the information required to evaluate the risks, the "what-do-I-have?" part, let alone the second part, the factors threatening whatever we have. Earlier we discussed the complex motivation of hackers and the complicated and rigid systems they can attack.

Given these, it is hardly surprising that the average user does not even know how they can protect themselves, if they can at all and are capable of doing so, and what protection measures are available. Of course, one defense strategy is to behave in a way that cannot get us in trouble or embarrass us if anything comes out, which seems a rather time-consuming solution. Just imagine writing every email in such a way as to make sure they could not harm us if disclosed. Attributed by the American public to North Korea, the hacker attack against Sony Pictures in late 2014 had the somewhat unexpected side effect of internal emails being disclosed in which management members made openly racist and sexist comments, actually naming the President of the United States and Hollywood film stars. But even if we are careful, this is not always effective and it is certainly insufficient by itself. Even those who pay their taxes properly do not want their tax details disclosed to everyone.

In November 2015 Charlie Sheen shocked the public by making a dramatic statement. He admitted to being HIV positive. When asked by the NBC News Today's reporter why he had decided to reveal this fact to the general public, he said that he had had enough of the dilemma in which he was caught between the problem of having to keep it secret or the problem of admitting it and dealing with the consequences of its disclosure. He had already paid millions of dollars to buy the silence of those who had been blackmailing him. The blackmailers included a prostitute who had used her smartphone to take a photo of the special medicine Sheen was taking for his condition and demanded money from the actor not to disclose the photos. Anyone who did not know about his illness but had had a sexual relationship with him might want to sue him for not telling them, although he insists that he did tell all of them. It is worth watching the interview videos as it is an excellent illustration of how an individual is torn when revealing his secrets, "letting them go." Sheen says that he did nothing to expose himself to particularly significant danger, in short: it was not his fault he got infected. And yet, he had to keep this secret. But what is the right decision in a situation of this nature? And for how long should a secret like this remain a secret? What date or objective can flick the secrecy-switch? And who decides in all of this?

There is an oft-used notion in data protection and in the legal practice of some countries: the idea of purposeful action. Data protection experts like to emphasize this expression, although defining and applying it presents quite a problem. Purposeful action essentially means that data can only be collected, stored, and managed about someone or something if this is done to achieve a particular objective. If, for example, the objective has not been achieved, then the data cannot be collected and managed either. Exactly what kind of data can be collected to reach a particular goal? How can we tell that in order to achieve a given objective we only deal with the data that we absolutely have to, i.e. that we have opted for the "best" way to tackle a problem? Only then can we address the most important question: will I keep to this? Facebook knows our name, gender, age, and educational background; it knows our personal and family relations, our friends, favorite films and music, our religious preferences, political views, and probably almost everything else. Such data can be matched, safely and legally of course, with user data outside Facebook through data broker companies like Epsilon. You could ask if all that data is collected and stored for advertisement purposes? And how does this relate to Facebook CEO Mark Zuckerberg's comments at the Crunchie award ceremony in San Francisco in 2010, that privacy is no longer a norm expected by society? And what's the connection between all this and Facebook's little blue dinosaur (Privacy Dino) who is supposed to be advising users how to take care of their private secrets? So, acting for a specific purpose is, unfortunately, not a strong enough argument on its own to successfully reduce risks in all cases.

In addition to or instead of purposeful action you can, of course, adopt general guiding principles governing data collection, but to apply such principles we need to know what kind of data we are dealing with. How can we establish what some information actually is unless we take a closer look? Do we opt for the legal route? It seems too slow and static a solution given the changes happening every day on the Internet. Should we ask users who these days do not even know what their personal data is and what not? Even if we receive an answer, we cannot "undo" having seen their data. This is the very same mechanism as when business partners send the wrong price list or address an email mistakenly. This is exactly what happened in 2014 when Goldman Sachs took legal steps to make Google delete an email from the Gmail account of a Google user, after the sender mistakenly addressed their message to a @gmail.com account instead of @gs.com, which is the official Goldman Sachs email domain. Even if it is deleted, you cannot undo it. Based on about 250 billion emails a year by 2020, and emails bouncing back due to wrong addresses accounting for about 1%, it is safe to assume that there could be roughly the same amount of misaddressed emails around by 2020, i.e. 2.5 billion a year.

Suppose we copy the Facebook model and collect data about everything and anything we can. This presupposes that we can build a system to collect all the data about all of us at all times with a particular purpose of drawing conclusions. As amazing and as lifelike a solution as this may seem, it would have clear consequences: the system would have to decide what should be done when it finds out about someone who has lived a licentious life as a syphilis patient in the past few months. There is no guarantee for the concealed nature and protection of such databases: they can be broken into, poked at, and leaked, and in fact, this is bound to happen. Yet we create these databases because they make our world more comfortable and we wouldn't be able to analyze real risks without them either. This irresolvable duality results in tension and increasing dilemmas that we cannot deal with. Projecting the "privacy vs security" dilemma onto our secrets.

So it's not only that even private individuals have quite complicated structures of secrets in their computers, on their phones or even on their kitchen worktops, but also that we are surrounded by those risky situations that we could in fact fix, or that we could avoid in the first place, provided we have the necessary information.

A tough question indeed. Who is to decide whether we can get a given piece of information or not? These days it is up to private individuals whether or not they choose to disclose that kind of information. But what if the private individual himself does not wish to divulge the information? Then are we not supposed to know?

Information security experts encounter variations on problems like this every day. It is important and urgent to find out about something, but you cannot ask the question until you have official authorization. But obtaining this requires acting with purpose, you need to explain why you are requesting the authorization.

If we knew in advance whether the writer of an email was reliable or not, we would think otherwise about the contents of the mail. To do so, we would need information to reduce our risk. In the case of an email, this means today that we read the name of the sender, which can be falsified in about 10 seconds, and the actual sender can essentially say whatever he chooses. Then we look at the subject line, which, again, you can change as you wish. Then we try to draw conclusions from the text. Some of the better service providers already provide some kind of protection against spam and viruses, but their efficiency is not 100%, given the fact they are struggling with the same problems as their users: they have no information so they try to obtain sufficient information from the elements of the emails and the various databases available to decide whether the given content is suspicious or not.

The blackmailing package Angler, which demanded ransom money from users for decoding encrypted electronic media, "generated" more than $30 million per campaign in 2015 and 2016. Some 10% of the millions of users targeted on a daily basis took the bait, and about half of them were infected; as a result, some of them were forced to pay to get their data back. All of this happened despite email screening services and products we had considered effective for more than 10 years, and users have been informed about ever since computer viruses first appeared. If a social media portal can tell what our favorite band is, what our political beliefs are, and whom we have been in love with, then why on earth can we not decide whether we can trust the sender of a virus-infected email or not? Again it's simply because we have no information about them, although somewhere, some service provider must know for sure who the sender of that mail is.

An interesting aspect of blackmailing and encoding viruses is that they make a secret out of our data that had not been secret before. As a standing – and nasty – joke among security experts says, a crypto virus actually encrypts our data for free. But at the same time the person who created that virus will cut us off from reading our own secrets, we will not have access to our own data and they are the one who will hold the key to our secret, not us. This clearly shows that secrets have a significant value, translated into money by blackmailers. Is it worthwhile then for a company or a private individual to pay tens of thousands of dollars to obtain those secrets? It seems that it is.

The need to track down the sender of malicious mail (e.g. a blackmailer) implies that we need to connect databases that we could not connect before, because without linking them to a purpose, we cannot keep the activities of everybody under surveillance. Or can we? Just remember the mammoth Facebook databases, the NSA tapping campaigns revealed by Edward Snowden or the Great Firewall project of the Chinese government which monitors all inbound or outbound communication of every internet user in the country. Why could we not connect a system of databases in this way for the purposes of enhancing our security and reducing our personal risk? The Apple vs. FBI debate over the decoding of a dead terrorist's phone was actually about finding a solution to this: to know what they are looking for, the FBI has to enter places they are not allowed to. Although the case has been solved, because the FBI found an alternative solution, Apple did not have to decode the phone, and so we have still made no progress in the fundamental question. In a similar case in the future we would end up at a similar deadlock. Given the quantity of data and the speed of connections, in the future it may be applications or computers giving the answer instead of individuals on a case-by-case basis, which could ground decisions about the disclosure of data on the basis of authorizations and global principles.

Applications that appear quite extreme today may take care of our health in the future. If someone takes out an insurance policy, and presuming therefore that the individual avoids risks like AIDS, then the IT system supporting his life insurance will have the right to view the health information of those other people who have had a sexual relationship with the person. And a light will flicker on your phone: "Watch out, your potential partner's health background is questionable or problematic," and the software will insist that you just forget about that intercourse because the person's insurance may not be able to cough up enough money for medical treatment if required, and they may even lose their policy.

The value of a secret is also defined by how much we want to spend on its protection, what consequences it will have if the secret is disclosed, and also to what extent this can be predicted. Today we analyze every secret ourselves, often without being aware of doing so, but we try to evaluate the risks of a secret getting leaked. In the future we might see programs and machines decide instead of us which data and information we should deal with and at what depth. They will process information for us and the software will know us well enough to pass on the information it knows we can process.

CHAPTER 10

CYBERSPACE: THE KILLER THEME PARK

"We'll be very careful, okay?"

When I first encountered the characteristic screens of the Internet in the early 1990s, now proudly described as "retro," I thought to myself, now here is something that will really change people. One could say anything on the internet because nobody knew who you were, allowing for total honesty under the cloak of anonymity. However, I did not consider the fact that the Internet had only been around for a few decades, while humanity has been undergoing development for millions of years. People are too smart to be honest. The opposite of what I was expecting actually occurred with regard to the Internet: people lie all the time online precisely because it is anonymous. And finally, it is not the Internet that has changed people, but vice versa: people have manipulated and twisted the Internet until it has become molded to their own desires.

The low credibility of cyberspace, and the security issues surrounding it, stem precisely from the fact that anybody can claim anything. Why couldn't someone claim that they have been on Mars? This behavior is primarily rooted in the fact that people actually lie to themselves more than anyone else. Knowing cyberspace, it is unrealistic to expect it to be the platform that showcases the road to self-knowledge where people can start discovering their true selves and understanding why they have been lying to themselves since the age of two.

The Famous Hungarian writer and poet Frigyes Karinthy describes this human trait by explaining that anybody can become an astronaut or Nobel prize winner, but people usually let go of these expectations and tend to lie to themselves less as time goes on. Until then, however, we are surrounded by a dual illusion of the world, one in which every employee is committed to fighting for the client's interest, where every baker is kind and every bun is made of purely healthy ingredients, every family is happy, every soup turns out delicious and every policeman is fair. This solution does not accommodate the fact that 28% of the police is corrupt; admitting such facts would make the illusion crumble. People, corporations and the state are actively engaged in maintaining this illusion. This is the reason why many official corporate missions and messages are worded so strangely and unrealistically.

This comforting illusion has been transplanted to cyberspace as well. Security issues, scams, password theft, bank card fraud, and data leaks, or just the difficulties of changing a password, erode this image of perfection. Maybe this is why we prefer not to notice. My father George is a renowned surgeon, one of the best in his field. I do not know anybody more conscientious, true to his profession and philanthropic than him. He has sacrificed a good part of his life to trying to explain situations to patients' relatives, what is going on or what is about to happen to their loved ones. He claims that the majority do not understand or grasp the situation because it is not happening directly to them, and because they often do not even comprehend what is being said to them. They keep responding along the lines of, "But he has looked so good so far. There was nothing wrong with him yesterday." Until people live through an experience themselves, my father always said, they do not learn — not even at the expense of others. He always asks me why I do not hack the systems of those that I'm trying to help, because then they would understand. I explained to him that just like he doesn't poison wells just to get patients, we do not hack something just to give ourselves work. "But then they will never learn, believe me, son." And he is right — they don't. I really wanted to avoid being the footsoldier sitting on the ground, broken, and with a sad wisdom in his eyes as he watches his fellows run into the enemy's trap despite his warnings. But it really seems like this is the case.

Soldiers are constantly running towards death, partly because their commanders do no act logically. Surveys show that nearly 80% of corporate executives are unsatisfied with their company's cybersecurity protection capacities. At the same time, less than 60% plan to allocate a higher portion of their security budget to cybersecurity. Typically, half of all organizations and companies do not increase their annual cybersecurity budgets at all. This area resembles environmental protection and world peace: everybody agrees that it is something that needs to be done, but when it comes to taking action, people feel that it is up to others to do so. In one of Scott Adams's Dilbert comics, the boss at a management meeting says to the attendees that the company's objective is to make the world a better place. When the employees try to argue with him, he adds," But not for everyone." Many people swear to God that they will update their antivirus license, but only proceed to do so weeks later or never.

Security is a hassle and cybersecurity is a hassle against invisible problems. Prevention seems like nothing more than an aristocratic pastime for those with enough time and money. "I do the absolute necessary", the average executive or patriarch thinks to himself. In cybersecurity, they think, "I have a firewall and antivirus software," therefore I am safe. Many continue to rehash the mantra that they learned in 1995 during the era of pimply teenage hackers and Windows macroviruses, back to when "January 1, 2000" T-shirts were still considered cool.

If someone wants to imagine what they will need today and what they can choose from besides these two technologies, the closest approximation would be to imagine the two Marvel superheroes Iron Man and Thor, as the antivirus software and the firewall respectively. Now, standing behind them, imagine all the other superheroes from Marvel and other comics, from the Fantastic 4 to Spiderman, and even the Hulk. Each one has a different superpower useful against a different enemy. Corporations can choose from log analysis software, rights management solutions, intrusion prevention appliances, solutions against advanced persistent threats (APT), vulnerability management software, and roughly another 20 to 30 categories. Individuals can choose from password managers, intrusion prevention software, encryption technologies, and a multitude of other solutions to effectively protect themselves.

Of course the task does not end here, because purchasing a piece of security is not enough; we must also be mindful of what our protection system has caught, what it wants to communicate, and of course, as the stakes rise and our increasingly valuable secrets enter the digital realm (whether we are talking about a corporation or an individual) we must respond more rapidly and efficiently.

So why don't we allocate sufficient human and material resources to security? Why don't we pay enough attention to it? Because we are not aware that we are treading in a danger zone, we do not feel the danger in our gut. If we put a person in an arena like the ones used in ancient Rome to host the mercilessly spectacular gladiator fights, they would know that they were constantly in danger of having the lions released on them, and then the hyenas, a tiger, the rhinoceros, and the elephant. Our sensations sharpen in such circumstances, and we fight for our safety and our lives.

Evolution has already taught us that in such a setting, we must focus on multiple things at once in a concentrated manner. We all have weapons at our disposal and have each other's back. However, we do not hold this same perception of cyberspace. Instead, we tend to view it as a theme park where nothing bad can happen to us apart from maybe getting a scare or two in the castle of horrors. We buy some popcorn, take a roller-coaster ride, and eat some cotton candy. Kids love it so much that they never want to stop. Then at night we go home and go to sleep. The lights also go out at the theme park. Everybody is happy. But cyberspace does not sleep at night, the roller coaster is full of malfunctions, and could fall apart at any moment, the weapons in the shooting gallery are live, pins have been hidden in the cotton candy, and it is only a matter of time before we walk into a hidden trap.

Cyberspace and everything that it contains are just like a dangerous factory, at least until security experts find a solution to keep careless users from getting into trouble. This remains a thing of the future. Just as we cannot buy a car without safety belts, we cannot use a smartphone without security measures. In cyberspace, more than 50% of data theft is aimed at using the stolen personal data, and nearly 25% is intended to cause actual material damage, or to put it more simply: to steal money from us. In 2015, nearly 20% of all data theft involved healthcare data. Databases containing users' bank, email, and website passwords are sold for thousands of dollars every day on the black market. These contain the data of individuals, citizens, and employees, which are stolen from average people just as much as from corporations or the state. This information constitutes the basis of our secrets. The time has come to foster individual attitudes towards this global issue that affects everyone, in those who still choose the path of ignorance.

CHAPTER 11

RESEARCHING SECRETS

*Cheating offline,
caught out online*

In light of the foregoing, the question of what people think today on the topic of secrecy is particularly interesting. The concept of secrecy has always been present in human communities: even before the handling of secrets was regulated by written or spoken laws. However, in both the concept of secrets and the handling of them, the approach to and most importantly, the regulation of secrets has always depended largely on the technological conditions of the era, its social structure, and many other circumstances.

Accordingly, the perceptions held by people regarding secrets, the fact and process of concealment, may have evolved over time — however, we do not have the means to gain insight into the attitudes of earlier populations. The question that must be asked today, in the second half of the 2010s, is: what do secrets conceal and how are attitudes toward secrets changing? This question retains its relevance over time, making it worthwhile to continue to investigate attitudes toward secrets in five, ten or more years. The differences can shed light on, among other things, the impact of technological development on the perception of secrecy, both on an individual and social level.

This research is qualitative, mainly based on the findings of in-depth interviews. It is aimed at investigating how people feel about the fact that the media deems secrets to be increasingly difficult to protect. In what areas of life do secrets occur most frequently? What types of secrets exist? Which secrets can be revealed to whom? When does something cease to be a secret? What are the consequences of revealing a secret? What is embarrassing, and what is dangerous to know? How are secrets different in the 21st century compared to before? How do secrets differ in the offline and online realm? The answers to these questions reveal numerous emotions and stereotypes; summarizing and organizing them would require much more space than is available here. So, for the sake of brevity, we will highlight the most common beliefs identified with regard to secrets.

Past and present

The interpretation of secret is constantly changing, both in time and across the social classes and strata of a given moment in time: *"Our definition of secret is undergoing constant change across historical eras, and perhaps even across social groups."* Moreover, individual perceptions within these groups also follow a development trajectory: *"Anyone who does not have a secret has never had a life; secrets stem from the past, that is where they originate."* Attitudes toward secrets are also very diverse on the individual level: *"It has become a sort of expectation to reveal secrets that we once strived to conceal, redefining the concept of what is a secret and what is not. As time goes on, we consider fewer things to be secret: what was once a secret no longer is."* Of course this also holds true in both the individual and historical dimension of time: *"How much money one earned was not a secret in the past, but it is today."* Besides the concept of secret, the process of keeping secrets has also changed: *"...today, it is easier for me to convey an image that is contrary to my actual wealth — if somebody wants to hide the fact that they are poor or rich, it is easily done today."* Individuals also have greater freedom in assessing the significance of a secret: *"If someone considers their secret serious, then it is serious for them, and if they consider it trivial, then it is trivial: I cannot decide for anyone else. There are secrets that I consider trivial, but which can spur others to seek out the ombudsman because of them. It is also society's task to empower individuals to decide for themselves which secrets are trivial and which are serious."*

Online and offline

In our era, it is new media — social media — that defines the nature of secrets: *"I want to keep myself hidden on the beach and on the street so that nobody can take my picture and post it online."* According to some people, the real and the virtual realms divide secrets into two groups, which nevertheless overlap at times: *"Our offline secrets can be revealed online: for example, François Hollande riding a scooter with his girlfriend."* The overlaps apply not only to secrets, but also to the people implicated in them: *"There are some contradictions. Some people cheat offline and get caught online. Others portray themselves as cool online, on Instagram or Tinder, but are bores in real life."*

Offline actions are unveiled online — this is one of the mechanisms of how secrets work. Meanwhile, other perceptions create a defining picture of the nature of secrets generated in the real and the virtual world. *"The current view holds that offline things carry more emotional value. This is not necessarily true. Online things are something that I think holds less emotional significance. Your girlfriend may not know that you are still using Tinder; this obviously has emotional significance. But offline secrets are usually more personal."*

The concept of control is closely tied to the borderline between real and virtual space: *"One can easily lose control of cyber-secrets, but the same holds true for offline secrets as well; for instance, having one too many drinks and revealing something that you shouldn't have. Nevertheless, one wields far greater control* over offline secrets than online secrets. In the online realm, whether your secret is stolen depends on whether anyone really wants to steal it and how concentrated an effort they make."

The perception of secrets generated and transformed in both real and virtual space elicited highly expressive, at times even poetic descriptions from respondents: *"Offline secrets are in a solid state. Meanwhile, online secrets are fluid, or even aerial. You pour it into a small something, a chat conversation, and it can end up anywhere. Nobody is needed for a secret to be revealed online, whether it be deliberately or inadvertently. If I have an offline secret and share it with you, then you would have to mess up for the secret to be revealed. However, none of this is necessary in the online realm, where information has a gaseous, independent life."*

Secrets of the virtual world can be classified into subcategories based on whether they originate from social or individual activities: *"If all of my emails and Facebook messages were publicly disclosed, I wonder how many secrets I would have left. Maybe quite a lot. I think I do not have that many secrets, and this may be something that I strive for. More things would probably be revealed about me if my Google searches were added."*

Access, secrecy, encryption

Access also shapes the situation of secrets. There are more secrets, but access to many of them is easier than before, when boxes holding secrets were buried in backyards. *"A lot of information,* the secrecy of which previously did not matter, is now easier to access... telephone lines are tapped, computers hacked, cell phones lost, making them accessible to people from whom one would prefer to hide them."

A new element of secrecy is encryption, which used to belong solely to the realm of IT experts just two or three decades ago, but has increasingly seeped into our daily activities: *"There is so much today on the internet, so much going on online that a lot of it needs to be encrypted. As the word itself suggests: anything that is encrypted becomes a secret concealed from the world."*

Emotions

The basis of secrecy is often fear: *"If anyone finds out, we will lose our competitive advantage, lose our image, contradict ourselves or incur a loss."* Fear may be motivated by a number of factors: *"We guard our secrets because we don't want to get caught."* The other aspect of fear is hope: *"Secrets are driven by fear and hope: fear that people will find out, and hope that they will not."* Fear is often generated not by the secret itself, but of the perception of it: *"There are some secrets that I don't even want to know. If I knew that a secret was dangerous, I would not want to know it."*

The group

The essence and nature of a secret is tied to some extent to the group that it relates to: *"Some secrets are about determining whom we can trust — a sort of test with unnecessary encryption."* This simultaneously ties the nature of the process of secrecy to the functioning of the group: *"Keeping secrets is adaptive. Whatever others conceal, I conceal as well, and the degree to which my friends keep secrets is the degree to which I keep secrets."* Moreover, it also defines the group itself in a certain sense: *"A secret is something that is defined relative to other people. A single person on a desert island cannot have any secrets."* What is and is not a secret between two people also defines the quality of their relationship: *"We strive to hide embarrassing things from most other people. But there are people who you are not embarrassed in front of, or feel that you know well enough are confident that it will not change their perception of you."*

The handling of secrets is also determined in relation to the group and the relationship: *"A secret is something that we deliberately keep from certain people. If my friend has a bad haircut, it is not a secret."* The same holds true for the impact of a secret: *"A secret is something that can impact multiple lives if revealed. We can look at this on a small scale, but it is not transparent because it would significantly impact the lives of one or more people if it were revealed. The secret is that I cheated on my girlfriend, so its revealing would have a greater impact, which we do not want to happen in the world, so we keep in under wraps."*

Privacy and publicity

The overlap and intertwining of the private and the public domain is clearly expressed in secrets: *"A lot of personal information can now be found online, or your telephone could be tapped, etc. A lot of these are things that people consider their personal domain and secret from the public at large. Many things that an individual considers to be secret hold no interest for the public."* This creates a level of indifference that is unfathomable for older generations, who were used to surveillance in the second half of the 20th century: *"I don't give a damn if our data is more exposed, because I know that nobody is curious about me. I don't have any secrets that I'm scared to death of being disclosed."*

And while during the aforementioned historical era, in the past 40 to 50 years, people would have wanted to know more about governments' intentions, today there is a sort of aversion or indifference regarding this as well. This is not synonymous with civil passivity, but shows that information about the workings of public administration and the media is increasing. *"Most state secrets are merely secrets because people are too stupid to grasp that on a grander scale, things need to be done that cannot be interpreted on an individual level, and these must be kept secret."*

Rationalization is also attested to by the fact that the process of interpretation groups things into types and categories: *"There are a lot of so-called state secrets that are not officially secrets, and are only concealed because there is nobody to expose them. People do not know where to look. This is the task of investigative journalism. Often these documents that should be officially published are not revealed, impeding investigative work."* Finally, there is a category of secrets that we know exist but have no intention of gaining knowledge of: *"Nuclear launch codes, now those can be dangerous."*

CHAPTER 12

LOOK, WHO'S SECURING NOW?

Everybody has secrets and every secret is of interest for somebody: the adventures of John Doe in the biscuit factory

The risks jeopardizing secrets must always be assessed, and we must live in a security-conscious way. The only problem is that this activity is so alien to most people that they choose to ignore it altogether.

The physical realm offers a good example. The average person does not like to think about the potential ways a burglar may get into his home, or to draw up a daily list of new weak points. "If the lock on my window is already old and loose, a burglar can easily push it in, so I will add buying a new window lock to my to-do list. Then, let me see, the bars on the door are also weak, and the lock jams often and is old; let me add that to my list as well. Let me make a few phone calls to the locksmith. Then there is the entrance to the building that can be opened with practically any key, so I will tell the building superintendent that the lock needs to be changed. The camera that I installed has gathered dust, so the infra-sensor might not detect a burglar; let me climb up and clean it." All of this sounds quite unrealistic, doesn't it? In the realm of IT, all of this is far more difficult because we do not see the weak points, and cyber burglars are also invisible, potentially located in any part of the world and relentlessly trying to break in. People understandably do not preoccupy themselves with these things: it is an ancient method of distancing ourselves from danger to avoid attracting it.

As the common man had few secrets in Europe during the Middle Ages, the concept of secrecy was often intertwined with mysticism. The term "secretist" was sometimes associated with alchemy. The 1828 edition of Webster's dictionary defines "secretist" as a "dealer of secrets," adding that the term is no longer in use. The definition can still be found in the 1844 and 1913 editions, the latter characterizing the term as obsolete. While dealers of secrets have become a forgotten thing of the past, secrets themselves not only remain present, but the modern age has introduced new phenomena. In his book *Proletarian Renaissance,* published in 1999, the renowned Hungarian sociologist Elemér Hankiss argues that the average man lives like a Renaissance prince, only without the castle. But if today's man wants to take a bath, he merely has to take a minute to open the faucet and let the water run, while the Renaissance prince had to wait for his water to be heated in a tub. Or if he wants to listen to some music, he can download his favorite songs in two seconds with no need to bring together a band and everything else that was necessary to convene in the garden and listen to live music. Not to mention food, transportation, and all the other comforts of modern life. So essentially, in many ways we have the same lifestyle as a Renaissance prince, even if we do not have the same wealth or castles.

In the past, secrets and information were the trappings of high status in the social hierarchy, but today, most people have an email address and a bank card, and watch online porn, compared to the relatively few princes who had naughty paintings adorning their walls. This means that everybody automatically has secrets, and quite a few at that. These include some that we are not even aware of, but nevertheless need to protect.

Meanwhile, there are other secrets that we would not understand even if we knew about them. Newborn infants have a tax number, and are examined from the time of their birth. These constitute the infant's own personal data and secrets. Any person, whether they like it or not, will have a wealth of data by the age of one week, and it would be unfortunate if anyone but his or her parents accessed this data. In a case in Utah, a woman's personal data was stolen and used in place of the actual data of the woman giving birth. So when the child's methamphetamine test came out positive, child welfare services contacted the victim of the data theft, and despite the fact that the case was solved and settled many years ago, she continues to receive information to this day about the condition of the child, who was never hers. Moreover, this information has become definitively intertwined for modern information systems.

In the wake of the restructuring and distribution surrounding data, a person amasses a huge amount of secrets by the age of 14. However, most of society is unable to handle this situation in the same way as those who possessed information and secrets in past eras. Although we have the comfort of Renaissance rulers, it seems we do not have all the necessary resources. Rulers had multiple advisers in charge of guarding all of their secrets and sensitive information, and these advisers generally had an interest in protecting their ruler. This is not an option for the modern private individual. We are alone with our secrets.

Just like our imaginary average citizen John Doe, who lives in a town called Tarbin, Pennsylvania and works at the local biscuit factory. When he begins his day at home, his first action is to browse his emails on his laptop. He receives three emails with malicious content that, if opened or viewed, release a cryptolocker, a ransomware virus that encrypts data stored on the computer, or allows a phisher to steal his bank card data. Meanwhile, his emails are also downloaded onto his smartphone, one of which contains trojan software that can steal all the numbers and personal information from his cell phone. So he has to remain focused on what he can open and what he cannot.

Let's assume that John has successfully navigated the digital email landmines, has not let loose any viruses, and has even checked his Facebook without clicking on any phishing advertisements. He then goes to work. The product development office is on the third floor of the biscuit factory, where John works on upcoming recipes. This is the unit that decides what ingredients to put in the biscuits to give them that unique, characteristic flavor that sets them apart from competitors, and gives them their hard and crunchy texture. Staff members send exact product ingredients, especially the PDFs containing the classification of harmful ingredients, between each other by email, so John must continuously stay focused on correctly typing email addresses to make sure that the secret recipes or studies on the health detriments of eating biscuits are not sent to an unknown Gmail inbox.

When browsing online, John must be careful to avoid catching a virus that can collect all of the sensitive information on his computer without his knowing it and send it out to competitors or hackers from his email cache, who can then blackmail the biscuit company.

Once he is done with daily tasks, or if he simply steps out for lunch for a sandwich — he has not been in the mood for biscuits for years — John needs to lock his computer to prevent anyone accessing and using it while he is gone. Once he gets home, he opens his computer once again and sees that it is the final deadline for submitting his tax returns, meaning he will have to spend some time on a website and an application. He has to make sure that when he logs into the tax platform, he is not on a fake website and does not transmit any personal information or tax information on this fake site. When John finally goes to bed and starts the sleep cycle monitoring function on his smartwatch, he must recall whether he has updated the watch's software, and if so, whether he has also done this for his intelligent bathroom scale synced with the watch. When he falls asleep, only the LED light of the internet router, protected by the same weak password for years, remains silently blinking in a corner of the room.

I have to admit, I do not envy John Doe — this is a lot for an average man. This is the private individual's perspective, the perspective of a citizen trying to preserve their own secrets; while at the same time he is also a corporate employee striving to protect the corporation's secrets. It is the same person, but the different roles call for slightly different behavior. John Doe's bosses in the biscuit factory, or the workers at the tax authority have a similar task, but have access to different secrets and also react differently in some cases. Their strategic objectives and methods differ at times, but they share the same mentality.

Everybody has plenty of serious secrets on their own individual level. Revealing any of these secrets in a given context could create serious problems. If somebody has total savings of $5,000 that they have been setting aside for five years in a bank account, and a hacker finds out where the money is kept and steals it, the harm done would be equivalent to that of a large corporation's customer database being stolen by cybercriminals. Everybody and everything has a secret that carries interest for another person, a company, a hacker, a terrorist, another state or even a robot. Secrets are system-independent.

The method that we use to protect our safety and attempt to guard our secrets in the cyberworld is to adopt a security-aware attitude. The promotion of vigilance — especially in the military and transportation — is rooted in history. During the second World War, it was prohibited to talk about the movements of military forces, their equipment, and the destination of ships, and there were poster campaigns reminding soldiers and the public of adhering to this safe behavior. "If you tell where he's going... He may never get there!" says an American wartime poster depicting a self-assured marine boarding a ship. Security-aware behavior is a relatively new concept in cyber security. National Cyber Security Awareness Month (NCSAM) was held for the first time in the US in 2004. Cyber security is a relatively young field that is constantly changing, with new concepts emerging and disappearing over the course of just a few years. Web Application Firewall (WAF) technology only lasted a few years, and we could also mention heuristic analysis or even the concept of virus itself, which has slowly changed over time and is now referred to using the broader term *malware*. At the same time, security-awareness has retained its status from the outset. Nevertheless, its value and utility seem to be undergoing erosion, because, despite efforts to instill security-aware attitudes in people, if they are not receptive to it and often forget what they are told, it is no surprise that people are no security experts. In addition, most software only supports a security-aware attitude to a small degree, and in most cases provide no warning if a user is about to act recklessly. Even cybersecurity experts or security companies have a hard time differentiating a malicious email from a safe one.

If there are too many cyber threats, poor John Doe cannot concentrate on passwords, pin codes, and updates every second while he is walking through a cybersecurity killing field, his security-aware attitude will seem irrational. We tend instead to rely on help from software, from experts, or from anybody we trust. In light of these facts, it would come as no surprise if the concept of security-awareness undergoes serious transformation and takes on new meanings and interpretation in the future.

CHAPTER 13

CORPORATIONS, *OHHH* CORPORATIONS...

Hackers behind oil barrels, data protection, romance in the sky, a bucket and a mug

If you believe that the level of security-awareness of a corporation or a government agency is higher than that of the average citizen, then go and get yourself a glass of water from the kitchen, pick up this book again, and take a deep breath. Most corporations have just the same practices as individuals. As the soldier from the old joke shouts from the trenches to the enemy: Don't shoot, there are people here!

Saudi Aramco is a Saudi Arabian oil company worth trillions of dollars, one of world's wealthiest corporations, with daily revenues in the ballpark of several billions of US dollars, and 55,000 employees, accounting for a large portion of the world's oil production. In 2012, it suffered one of the worst hacker attacks of all time. In May of that year, one of the company's IT workers opened an email that he shouldn't have and hackers managed to infiltrate the system. On August 15 (during Ramadan) Aramco users encountered strange phenomena on their computers: unexplained shut-downs and disappearing files. A hacker group claimed responsibility for the attack, which was staged in opposition to the oppressive regime of the Al Saudi royal family that Aramco was a supporter of.

The attack was so successful that the company's employees ripped out the network cables from all existing computers and servers across the world, and Saudi Aramco was propelled back to 1970s technology, using typewriters and faxes. Even the telephone lines were down in many locations. A few weeks later, the corporation started giving oil away for free within Saudi Arabia in an effort to retain its market position. The situation went on for months, while the company bought tens of thousands of new hard drives and computers to relaunch its IT operations.

Fast forward ahead four years in time. At a Middle Eastern airport in May 2016, the following conversation takes place with an employee of an oil company:

Cybersecurity expert (CE): I remember that awful attack; those must have been hard times!

Employee (E): Indeed, it was horrible. It was very stressful.

CE: I presume that the lessons were learned.

E: Very much so.

CE: What has changed? I assume that security is now more of a priority.

E: Not really. As a matter of fact, things are just like they were before.

And this is the essence of the matter. Even such a devastating attack failed to overwrite oil company security practices. We might assume that, surely, users are just unable to see behind the scenes and in fact, everything has changed, but in terms of security-awareness, it is the *people* who are essentially responsible for a lot of things. In 2012, it was an IT expert who let the virus in, and the same thing may very well occur in 2020.

Corporations allocate 5% of their IT development budget to security. Or do they? Estimates vary and it is hard to gauge the actual figure. According to the SANS estimate, corporations spend between 4-6% on cyber security in relation to total IT investments. Roughly 2.5% of companies spend over 25%, while 15% of companies spend less than 3%. The latter category has decreased over the past three years, while the ratio of those allocating 4-12% is on the rise. This is a positive sign.

At the same time, the ratio of companies spending a large chunk of their budget (between 1 and $10 million per year) is dwindling. Once corporations see that no matter how much money they channel into security, they will still have a hard time successfully decreasing the number of attacks, they ask themselves how much is enough. An average business decision-maker can be convinced in a matter of 1.5 seconds to invest less in an area that does not directly generate profit. No matter how much we spend on security, a lack of awareness will always counter our expectations.

If the objective is to identify what areas to pay attention to and the levels of security within the company, a good method is to learn from past incidents. If information has been leaked from the organization in the past as a result of human error, it can provide an indication of the company's level of security-awareness. However, the indicator is not completely representative and cannot be applied to the entire company. It is like walking up to a few passersby on the street and asking them about the average level of welfare in the country.

Corporations also use employee questionnaires as a method. An example may include a question popping up when workers turn on their computers in the morning: "Are you allowed to leave your company laptop in your car while you go swimming? Yes/ No." This requires a response before the user is allowed to access their computer. Although these methods are more successful, nonetheless, just as a capuchin monkey is able to learn how to open a twist-cap bottle in a matter of two minutes, people can also easily learn how to respond quickly to security questions. The monkey has merely accessed the fruit hidden in the bottle, and the human has accessed their computer. However, their security-awareness has not necessarily increased by any degree.

An additional problem is the security-awareness of IT experts themselves. An IT expert has noticed that one of the systems he operates is vulnerable, or that the hackers of another country's government have been hiding in his database for years; what does his security-consciousness tell him? Should he report the case? Will he be fired because of it? And what exactly should he report? Because experts often cannot clearly gauge what is true and what is not of a cybersecurity event. From inside. From where the crime was committed. There is no corpse or smoking gun. Only a secret. How long should it be kept concealed? Perhaps he should resolve the issue himself?

It is not uncommon for system operators to immediately address an identified flaw during routine checks by security experts, to avoid being accused of having overlooked something. Abracadabra! There is no security issue here, ladies and gentlemen. Everybody can go home, and our jobs will be safe.

For this very reason, these impacts drive many discussions on the lack of information between communication, IT and legal experts within large corporations. Someone always asks the uncomfortable question: "Guys, I don't know what to tell people. Just tell me what happened exactly." The IT expert generally throws up his hands: "You have to understand that I cannot explain what happened, because I don't have all the data. I did not receive it, and don't have proper insight into what is happening. I don't know whether or not the data was stolen. Plus it is not my fault; we did not buy any new security solutions." In a 2016 study, social researchers from the University of Maryland investigated the models of crisis communication. Their key advice was that best practice consists of recognizing and communicating uncertainties to avoid getting caught in a lie or exaggerating.

Missing information, when combined with the uncertainty of security-awareness, creates a state where any number of decision-makers can think for as long as they want about what happened. None of this, however, will make up for poorly planned or nonexistent protection systems, the resulting lack of information and the general absence of a security-aware attitude. I do not envy the work of large corporate communication professionals during times of cyber attacks aimed at their company.

One might think that this suggests a failure of raising security-awareness. But raising organizational or collective awareness of cybersecurity is a difficult matter, because few people are able to think on the level of an entire collective's security and to put themselves in the shoes of the community's collective mentality. Most people place a greater priority on their own interests and secrets, as opposed to those of the whole group.

Although humans are capable of sacrificing themselves for the community, the evolution of group dynamics has not yet reached the stage where we are able to fight like a lioness for her cubs, to protect the secrets of others. In other words, we will not tackle hackers if they steal the company's data. Perhaps we need more time for data, information and the development of collective secrecy to gain sufficient value for it to be internalized by individuals. For those who work with such data, they need to understand that the value of what they are holding in their hands is equivalent to the value of their health, their clothing or their life. Perhaps in the future, there will be measurable group characteristics to measure collective security-awareness.

Everybody wants to avoid data leaks. Projects aimed at preventing leaks are driven by the organization making the firm assertion: Enough, our data should not be leaked. However, this assertion never lacks the same fundamental driving force: behind every project of this sort is one or more data leaks that have already occurred. But the clock is ticking. Most data leak issues and the lessons learned remain topical for two or three months. Then they are quickly forgotten, like a bad memory. If nothing can be done to make IT systems more secure during this period, it will be useless later on because nobody will remember that the problem even existed, and as a direct consequence, nobody will be willing to sacrifice either money or energy.

If a data protection project is launched, potential data leak issues must be interpreted on a far broader scale than warranted by the incident that triggered the measures, in order to provide the most comprehensive protection possible. However, the first challenge arises right from the outset: executives are often unable to gauge the relative importance of a lot of things, they don't truly understand which secrets are the most valuable for the company and so they are unable to provide relevant input for the project.

The head of security of a large bank recently complained to me: "The truth of the matter is that we have been wanting to introduce effective protection against data leaks for a long time. But the introduction of every project of this sort begins by identifying which data is confidential and which is not, and their respective classification and level. Somebody should know what keywords to search for in our system to know whether something can be sent out or not."

Let me confess a white secret. Once on a flight, I found one of the air hostesses very attractive. I would like to say that this has surely happened to all of us, but people are loathe to confess such things, like watching porn, burping or staring at accidents. Open intelligence is also an available option; nobody ever got into trouble by poking around online, I thought. I began with the most classic source of community information, Facebook; unsurprisingly, it is the first source that many social engineers, hackers, and secret service experts seek out when collecting information. Since Facebook expanded its search services to broader topics in 2015, using its search function has become a piece of cake.

The search started out innocently enough, but what I discovered was shocking. I found the airline's Facebook page, but not the official content that I was expecting. Instead, I had landed on a special page managed by flight attendants, with around 8,000 members dedicated to exchanging flight schedules along with their names, photos, personal information, and often telephone numbers. If a particular flight does not suit somebody's schedule or they want to cancel something, they simply switch with a colleague willing to take on the flight. The page lists the staff on specific flights, along with crew photos snapped with a telephone from the airline's system. The attentive surfer not only encounters a multitude of interesting internal codes and technical terms, but can also decipher the internal mobile application used by employees based on the screenshots posted on the page. Most surprising, all of this is in a fully open group, with the data of all members publicly accessible and searchable by name.

Publicly disclosing such information carries a considerable security risk. Without giving anyone ideas, I will simply present the facts. The open Facebook group reveals the flights that every flight attendant will take, including dates and destination, flight number, as well as the technical jargon used by the company, the operation of the mobile applications used and the name, photo, and telephone number of every staff member. These can all pave the way for a successful cybercriminal attack or even a physical attack, as the data on display is essential information. Okay, but what happened to the pretty air hostess? I found her in the group, we met and got married one year later. We have two beautiful children and a cute Dalmatian, and live in our California home. But in fact, no, I did not manage to find her. I do have a dog though.

Similar unofficial corporate groups can be found in large numbers on social media websites. There are also open groups where former employees of companies go to gossip about current management or to exchange current personal information, listing real people, events, and times. Although reading such pages must be a form of joyful therapy for bitter ex-employees, it is also a goldmine for tax authorities, economic law enforcement, data protection organizations, and cyber criminals.

Most people treat cybersecurity just like any other occupational safety training course. How much will it affect them personally? There will never be a fire here. The elevator will never get stuck. The security of access is not a "community task" either, so a social-engineer seeking to infiltrate an organization using Kevin Mitnick's methods begins by buying a company mug, filling it up with coffee, walking up to one of the employees smoking outside near the company, and engaging in conversation with them. At larger corporations, people do not know each other, as it is impossible to know everyone within such a large organization, so he will easily initiate a conversation, especially if he is holding the mug, because then he is certainly not a random stranger. Famous Hungarian Jewish publicist and humorist László Tabi wrote a satirical monologue entitled "What is a bucket capable of?" in which he recounts how he escaped and walked home from a work camp on the eastern Russian front with a bucket in his hand. He walked nearly 1,700 kilometers from Voronezh, Russia to Szolnok, Hungary. He was not stopped by a single patrol, control point or policeman, as they saw the bucket in his hand and thought that he must be going somewhere to get water. One must never underestimate the power of objects in manipulating people. An intruder holding a company mug in his hand will most certainly be able to walk with ease through the company's doors, and the doors will most likely be opened for him, no questions asked. It doesn't matter if he has an access card or not.

Imagine yourself in the shoes of an employee. Here is a nice young man with a mug in his hand. Should we start questioning his identity? It is not our responsibility, let alone our profession. We didn't choose the profession of security guard precisely because we don't want to deal with such things. So what should we do? "Fine, I see the mug in your hand, but could you please introduce yourself?" Plain embarrassing. Are we expected to start demanding to know people's identity? And if there are several, should we inspect each one of them? Can an employee be expected to voluntarily engage in such conflict? When the sun is shining, he is drinking his coffee, everybody is nice, who wants to start an argument? Moreover, most people tend to avoid conflict and triggering such situations. Nobody wants to create tension or assume responsibility. This is why manipulation is effective: this is why relying on security-awareness does not work adequately.

CHAPTER 14

ARE YOU LACKING SECURITY-AWARENESS? TRUST SOCIETY!

*We here at Society
will solve your problem.*

It seems that security-conscious behavior does not come easily for either private individuals or companies. Leave it up to society to unite and resolve the issue, one would think. This however, will only lead to disappointment: humans are not ants and often act more thoughtlessly in large groups than when alone.

For a start, let's look at the self-appointed justice-serving, summary judges of cyber security: the Anonymous hacker group. This group is neither a corporation, a state, nor a private individual, but a group of civilians, who are sometimes very right, and sometimes very wrong.

But as a group, its members behave differently than as individuals. Members are spurred to take action, and private individuals go into battle and do what they have to: they hack websites, publicly disclose data, and reveal secrets to the public at large. This is called hacktivism. We could even refer to the Anonymous group as digital society's security and cyber conscience, while others simply consider them cyber terrorists or uncontrollable cyber scum. Since the assumed establishment of the divisive group in 2003, it has disclosed immense volumes of data, taken on the church of Scientology, the Ku Klux Klan, and ISIS, unmasked several terrorists, and wreaked havoc for major global organizations such as Sony, PayPal or the New York Stock Exchange.

Irrespective of whether or not their actions, carried out with good intentions, truly serve the general good, Anonymous do unmask secrets. They disclose secrets to allow society to be the judge. They generally hold a mirror to their victims, denude them, and then leave it up to different groups of society to make a judgment. The secret is often that the victim is a hypocrite, claiming to be something that they are not. In the realm of concealment, this is often the extreme of gray and black secrets, the area that we most want to keep hidden.

But the actions and methods of the Anonymous group, and the secrets they have disclosed, compel society to relativize: it is difficult to decide what is true and what is not from what we hear and see. And this leads us back to the question of the degree to which we can trust digital evidence. In other words, there is a sort of social security consciousness that would like to see evidence that an unveiled secret is really what it appears to be. No matter how effectively the Anonymous group works, its own credibility may erode the value of the delivered secrets.

The Ghost Security Group was set up in 2014-2015 to address this very issue, founded by members of the Anonymous collective who deemed themselves more reliable, setting themselves the objective of fighting ISIS. The group was particularly active at the time of the Paris attacks in January 2015. They announced a "new kind of anti-terrorism" where hackers would side with justice, analyze data, collect information on terrorist cells, and help the world. So a network of trust has been woven around the spirit and hacker activities of Anonymous, thereby strengthening the credibility of the information disclosed.

In early 2016, a growing number of hacker sources started criticizing the group's activities, claiming that GSG was motivated by money and involved in dealing with information through an existing consulting firm. This shows the high levels of uncertainty prevailing in the cyber world, and how easily credibility can be compromised.

The Snowden scandal showed that society is slowly starting to grasp that we must somehow protect our secrets more effectively. In May 2013, Edward Snowden blew the whistle on the NSA's surveillance practices and on the information held by the organization, but his allegations were seriously called into question even by cybersecurity experts. Since then, Snowden's revelations have been confirmed to be true and this has largely improved the credibility of leaked data worldwide. Complete procedures, processes, and software have since emerged to leak corporate, state, tax, and private secrets, to be judged by society. SecureDrop is an open-source software and hardware solution that assists communication between data leakers and the press.

Society's security-awareness seems to be functioning well, but it assesses the information obtained only slowly and in an unpredictable way. For instance, if Sony claims that it has not been hacked because it has managed to avert an attack, then society, the gaming public, and the professional public will respond the same way in cyber cases as it would in other domains: wanting to believe the words of a credible company.

They want to believe the company is telling the truth because the company is considered an accepted protagonist according to social norms. We want to believe the company, and this is what economic rationality dictates in a normal economic setting. But as time goes by, and more and more information is disclosed, an internal email or two are leaked, confidential information published by hackers, secrets are revalued, their value will change and the situation may change. Society may end up believing the hackers. In the early 2000s, most of society blindly believed anything they were told by the FBI, the NSA or the government to be undoubtedly true. This is no longer the case today.

CHAPTER 15

THE DEEP-CLEANSING POWER OF THE PUBLIC

*Leaking to address stubborn stains,
bug bounties for pollutants, and a booster
for the cyber immune system*

So there is no other choice but to trust the power of the public and we must rely on global security consciousness — assuming that such a thing exists — to know that our secrets are safe. So now let's look up to the sky, touch our hands together, and from our combined powers, Captain Cyber is born. He gives governments a rap on the knuckles for censoring the internet and juggling with hackers, slaps hacktivists in the face, smacks global corporations upside the head to stop profiling their users, and saves the cyber kitten stuck in the tree. Sadly, we will still have to wait for Captain Cyber, because no one wants or is able to summon him.

But the power of the public is potent enough on its own even without any superheroes. Edward Snowden's only source of protection — later coupled with the Russian state who gave him refuge — was the public, without which he would currently be undergoing interrogation in the basement of some country or institution. Similarly, Wikileaks boss Julian Assange uses the same means when he addresses the public from the Ecuadorian embassy in London.

The scope, quantity, or quality of leaks can exert a considerable effect. Each individual action is measured in gigabytes — or sometimes just a few emails with high-impact content. Either way, they are forces to be reckoned with. Like the July 2016 issue of DC Leaks, which exposed the hacked emails of the former supreme commander of NATO forces in Europe, Philip Mark Breedlove. These emails revealed the commander's opinions about a military solution to the Russian-Ukrainian crisis, and about President Obama's and Angela Merkel's conflict-averse attitudes. The emails also reveal that the commander was fully in support of NATO's active but covert intervention in the conflict: Poland would have happily supplied weapons in secret to the Ukrainians if NATO were willing to become engaged in the conflict behind the scenes. In the past, such information was revealed not months or years after the fact, but decades later, thanks to the efforts of committed historians.

The impact of the public affects the average man just as much. If somebody presents themselves as a law-abiding citizen and ethical employee at work, but his friends regularly post compromising pictures of him out partying during the week on Instagram or Twitter, he will sooner or later be exposed by his mid-morning yawns before coworkers and family. He cannot pretend to be something that he is not: he cannot hide things that were formerly private.

The public eye changes transparency. In the meantime, the structure of the public has also changed and become more complex. These two impacts together have reduced the number of secrets that can be kept private. Hundreds of years ago, our taxes or correspondence were not public because most people simply did not pay taxes or write letters. At an event held in Eastern Europe, chief federal deputy and general counsel to the Utah Attorney General, Dr. Parker Douglas, explained how numerous cases are closed by searching Facebook and looking at targets' public photos, which often reveal evidence for the crime being investigated. The incriminating photos are saved and the case has been solved. In one environmental protection case, the defendant posted a photo on his own social media that shows him vandalizing protected rocks in the desert. He is doing exactly what he was under investigation for. This wrapped up the case in less than ten minutes. Open source intelligence (OSINT) has long been a part of the toolkit used by intelligence, police, law enforcement agencies and cyber security companies, but precisely because our secrets are increasingly exposed, hackers are also quick to use this method.

The changing transparency of our private lives has fueled the desire to reinforce our privacy rights. Dani Mathers, the 2015 Playmate of the year, snapped a selfie in the locker room of a gym, capturing a nude woman in the background and making derogatory comments about her, in the summer of 2016. The impact of the photo was huge and sparked a severe backlash against Mathers, who then deleted the picture from her Twitter, Instagram and Snapchat accounts. The gym franchise — citing its own policy and the law — banned the model from their gyms, and there were public rumors of litigation and judicial proceedings.

The protection of private secrets and privacy are becoming increasingly important in legislation as well. The topic is hard to define because, as we have seen, the protection of personal data, i.e. the protection of information, is not equal to the protection of secrets. In other words, no matter how well we protect our data, our secrets are far more complex. Nevertheless, the Privacy Shield to be created between the European Union and the US seems like a great initiative and will define how the data of EU citizens is handled when it leaves EU territory and ends up in the hands of, say, an American service provider. Although the US invests millions of dollars in cybersecurity and has far surpassed Europe in this regard over the course of the last few years, the individualistic attitudes prevailing and the commitment to private secrets in Europe has created a stricter regulatory model on the old continent. These laws, provisions and attitudes aimed at protecting privacy may set a good example for less individualistic states such as some Asian countries. The big question, however, is whether groups, religious communities and countries driven by community cultures have any need at all for the privacy of their members or citizens.

In addition, *the public* means something else from one place to the next. In 1998, China launched its golden shield project in the context of which the Great Firewall of China, i.e. China's Internet firewall, was created. It seems that humanity has always used large walls to control or protect great masses, whether in 200 BC or 2000 AD. The current Chinese defense system supervises the Internet traffic of nearly 1.4 billion internal inhabitants. Moreover, its activities affect the entire internet, as it was revealed in 2015 that all traffic passing through the wall (including incoming traffic to China) is under surveillance, and the system gives instructions to the browsers of external users to attack political targets, in other words the substantial cyber security infrastructure is not only used for protection, but also for initiating attacks. This portion of the system has been coined the Great Cannon. The use of encrypting VPN channels is prohibited within China's borders. If anyone attempts to use these, mobile operators disconnect them from the network — and this is the least that might happen to them. Even professor of IT Fang Bixing — referred to as the father of the Great Wall — had no choice but to attempt to create an encrypted connection when he was unable to reach South Korean websites during a university lecture.

Foreigners regularly report how once on Chinese territory,

their services disappear, they are unable to access their inboxes after a few hours, once the system has spotted them and restricted the available online services. China has developed its own services for its internal market, so the Chinese public does exist in this sense, but fundamentally differs from the public in the Western sense. Particularly in terms of the fact that the Chinese government monitors all services and communication, collects pertinent data and even analyzes it. Privacy in the cybersecurity sense does not exist in China, and we can be sure that Chinese users have a very different security-consciousness than American users.

Another undeniable trait of the public is its simplicity. The public has a hard time understanding complex, difficult matters, is incapable of understanding correlations in their true depth, and is quick to judge. Just like the top executive in the movie *Margin Call*, John Tuld, portrayed by Jeremy Irons and inspired by two key protagonists of the economic crisis, John Thain of Merrill Lynch and Dick Fuld of Lehman Brothers. In the movie, Tuld turns to the analysts, who have offered a prediction of the economic crisis using complicated formulas: "Maybe you could tell me what you think is going on here. And please speak as you might to a young child... or a golden retriever. It wasn't brains that got me here I can assure you of that."

In order for the public's security awareness to be able to understand the extreme complexity of cybersecurity, as described over multiple chapters in this book, it must be simplified. Like John Oliver, who asked Edward Snowden when interviewing him *not* to explain the systems created by secret services to survey citizens, but whether the spies were able to see dick pics or not. But simplification carries the risk that the public will not fully grasp the significance of security, and will not understand the consequences of ignoring cybersecurity. A simplified translation of the state of cybersecurity may easily result in most people not having a full understanding of it due to a lack of IT skills, but also because they simply do not want to make the effort, while there is a lot to understand.

There were rumors that the perpetrators of the 2015 Paris terror attacks used the PlayStation gaming console to communicate. Thousands of reports covered the topic and hundreds of cybersecurity experts were interviewed across Europe to explain how this could be possible. Public opinion wanted to hear solutions to avoid terrorists from using gaming platforms to communicate.

But the truth was something different entirely. What happened was that not long before the terrorist attacks, Belgian home affairs minister Jan Jambon said that security experts had a hard time deriving communication encrypted using a Playstation 4. Forbes reporter Paul Tassi misinterpreted the minister's words and linked the planning of the attack to the PlayStation network.

The interesting thing in cyberspace, and in the Internet as a communication channel, is its diversity coupled with its extreme rapidity. The veracity of a piece of news can be checked and verified relatively quickly and with a high degree of certainty.

If three or four leading online news sites or professional sites, perhaps on several continents or backed by different economic interests, publish the same piece of news, then it is likely to be genuine. This holds true for the cyber attacks that make the biggest ripples, because the outcome will sooner or later be communicated by the hacker or the perpetrating group. In several countries, companies are required by law to report incidents to a smaller or broader audience.

However, the case is less clear with regard to data leaks or data theft. If rumors emerge that somebody's email account has been hacked and several gigabytes of information obtained by hackers, such reports will have little credibility. Such events still remain mystical and incomprehensible for the public. The official announcement of an incident without any knowledge of the incentive and motives of the attackers only creates a guessing game and most people just shrug their shoulders. A prime example of this was the Anonymous group's Operation KKK, also known as #OpKKK, which leaked a list of 1,000 Ku Klux Klan member names in October 2015. The group posted the list on its Twitter page, but deleted it soon after and distanced itself from the incident. #OpKKK still theoretically exists to this day and continues to spark rumors from time to time, but the public has a hard time interpreting this domain and has lost interest in it.

An even more uncertain type of news, from the public's perspective, occurs when an IT device or system is revealed to be vulnerable. A straightforward way of explaining what is really going on (which may anger technical staff): IT experts and program developers design poor quality software and hardware as a result of negligence, lack of knowledge, or yielding to business pressure. So the flaws remain in the devices, and in large numbers at that: between 15 and 50 for every 1,000 rows of code, adding up to potentially thousands per device. The good, the bad, and the ugly hackers all reveal these flaws. The sky is the limit to the number of such vulnerabilities, with about ten new security breaches revealed per day, adding up to 20,000 new vulnerabilities per year, and we often do not know how long these vulnerabilities have been present. The well-intentioned hackers who report a security flaw to the company responsible for it may be in for a nasty surprise. They often find themselves face-to-face with the company's entire "military" arsenal, from the tenth dan legal department to the marsh crocodiles, all set on silencing the hacker in order to make the problem go away. There are of course some honorable exceptions. The situation begs for a clear and fair procedure for disclosing vulnerabilities to the public and other stakeholders.

Why is it a problem if we say that something is flawed? On one hand, if a software or device is already completed, then why pick it apart instead of being happy that it works? On the other hand, correcting flaws often creates other flaws, sometimes ones that may influence the basic functioning of the device, ruining "everything" that was good until then. In addition, correcting flaws is time-consuming, does not introduce any new functions or features and requires companies to explain themselves, or, to put it in economic terms: customers do not care. As a result, companies easily convince themselves that correcting flaws is an unnecessary hassle. Meanwhile, security experts tend to exhibit perseverance and asceticism that would put the Spartan 300 to shame, so they generally do not back down that easily. Especially because the phrase "it works" for a hacker is synonymous with the assertion that they cannot make it break. So if a hacker has reported a flaw but does not want to take on crocodiles and legal teams, the hostile reactions of corporations or state organizations puts even the most bona fide hacker in a difficult position. The choice is merciless. Should I take advantage of what I found in the hopes of attracting attention at the cost of being unethical? Or should I sell the vulnerability for money? Although this is not necessarily illegal, it is far from being ethical since who knows what the information could be used for. Or should I make it public at the risk of becoming the target of attacks and defamation, ending up as the bad guy? Should I maybe remain silent, allowing the flaw to claim many victims, because if I found it, then others will too, and they will exploit the flaw? Not to mention the other, even more unpleasant alternatives.

Luckily, more and more companies and manufacturers have realized that searching for flaws themselves is far more costly than leaving it up to the community or the public. Obviously, this calls for a regulated approach. This is referred to as responsible disclosure, which is not nearly as complicated as it sounds. In essence, developers, IT experts, software and hardware manufacturers and the companies that use IT products agree that neither protagonist will go too far. The battlefield must be regulated, nobody should use live weapons, and the reigning currency is money. In other words, companies launch what is referred to as bug bounty programs in the context of which they reward security experts, hackers or anybody who identifies a flaw within their system and reports and handles it according to the defined rules; this is what renders the process responsible.

In return, the companies also commit to addressing the flaws. It would be quite embarrassing if the same flaw remained on a wholesaler's website for two years, unresolved, and as the money has already been used up in the context of the bug bounty program, successful flaw hunters were rewarded with company pens and T-shirts. The Netherlands are pioneers in this area, with representatives of corporations, communities and the Dutch government having signed a declaration on the responsible disclosure of security flaws in early 2016. Such agreements generally go above and beyond the regulation of bug bounties and regulate the circumstances on all sides, laying down a clear procedure of when, how, who, and what can be disclosed. The agreement was signed at the High Level Cyber Security Meeting held in the context of the Netherlands' EU presidency. At a round-table discussion, a Dutch bank even reported that its bug bounty program had been successfully operating for a while, drawing several reports on the vulnerabilities identified within its systems on a weekly basis.

This reveals a new facet of the public and creates value, which is expressed through new phenomena, where the average person can show what they are capable of and do something for the community's cybersecurity. Social researchers can no longer call a hacker narcissistic for posting daily selfies with new vulnerabilities on his blog. This is a novelty. We might assume that a new and exciting capacity is in the process of emerging: the public's *cyber immune system*. Hackers, security experts, and the broader public are becoming sensitized to broader dimensions of security matters, and although the public often reacts in a knee-jerk manner, security-awareness nonetheless seems to be becoming instilled in certain groups. Even if we fail to find evidence suggesting that cybersecurity will become fundamentally ingrained in individuals and society anytime soon, perhaps this time, the public will be wiser than the individual. To quote George Orwell: "If large numbers of people are interested in freedom of speech, there will be freedom of speech, even if the law forbids it; if public opinion is sluggish, inconvenient minorities will be persecuted, even if laws exist to protect them."

CHAPTER 16

DO WE NEED
TO WORRY NOW,
GANDALF?

*Information and secrets
burned by spontaneity*

In *Kung Fu Panda*, when some bad news is brought to the wise Grand Master Oogway, the old turtle lifts his gaze and calmly says, "There is just news. There is no good or bad." Upon hearing the news, he responds: "That *is* bad news."

When you list all the security risks that have emerged in cyberspace in the wake of the radical changes of the 2000s, you are likely to elicit the same reaction. The growth in speed and data quantity, the receding of privacy, the disappearance of secrets, and many other factors have been addressed in previous chapters. Meanwhile, other phenomena are still in the embryonic stage but even now they are no better looking than the "facehuggers" familiar from the *Alien* movies, nestled in their eggs and waiting for their victims.

We have already addressed the issue of incorrect email addresses or emails that get lost on the way. A more severe case of information "gone awry" is the spontaneous mix-up of information in cyberspace. This is comparable to asking for no sugar in your coffee at Starbucks and ending up with somebody else's chai latte. Such mistakes are easily made in IT. By changing just one variable, we can magically end up in somebody else's email inbox. Users do not notice the fact that only a fine line separates them from other users when taking care of their finances online, sending emails, or making online purchases. This argument will surely anger web portal and target application developers and operators. Obviously, a well-designed application cannot mix up data and user profiles that easily.

But the fact of the matter is: yes it can. And increasingly so. The complexity of systems and the sheer quantity of data carry the inherent risk of this happening; not to mention the increasingly autonomous behavior of information technology systems, which slow down, accelerate, reconfigure, and update themselves. We are standing on the brink of the spread of self-repairing systems and learning mechanisms, already existing in a limited number of applications, and soon to become the mainstream. From there, artificial intelligence is just one step away.

So the spontaneous mix-up of information is a real and serious threat to cyber security, particularly as regards our more valuable and substantial secrets, such as our intimate photos or black secrets. We can never be entirely sure that one of these will not land "inadvertently" in third-party hands. Several symptoms of this phenomenon giving reason for concern have already emerged. Some users have reported that the popular online communications service Viber, which offers cheap messaging and voice services, simply mixes their friends' profile pictures with those of complete strangers. I have seen with my own eyes how my own father's profile picture was replaced by a young boy waving a German flag with the inscription "Polizei," and a few weeks later, by an unknown infant who slowly started growing, with monthly cameos from a total stranger taking care of the child. I am well aware of the fact that Viber pairs individual identifiers with users' cell numbers, so the phenomenon might have stemmed from an association issue between user profiles and a change in telephone numbers, and I could very well have investigated the matter. But I was just not interested in doing so. This is not the user's task. When I receive a message or call for my own father, I see the image of an infant and her father, people who I have never met. Although I myself do not care, they are probably not even aware of the fact that their intimate moments are displayed on a complete stranger's cell phone. I can only hope that the profile pictures will remain focused on the baby.

There is also the case of another popular application, Dropbox. This file-handling and filesharing application allows users to access their own data from multiple platforms. I was baffled when an IT system engineer and colleague of mine showed me how for the past year, photos of a complete stranger have been popping up among his own images on his device. The mix-up occurred in the file library where photos can be uploaded directly from smartphones and other devices. The images show general and more personal moments from IT people's meetings. Needless to say, this should definitely not be happening. It raises the question: who else can see the photos that we upload to Dropbox?

Something similar has already occurred in the field of web portals too. In early 2009, a user of the Hungarian online tax system — accessible through a government website dedicated to citizen administrative matters — found a link in an email sent by the system that gave him access to the tax information of an entirely different person. Their user contexts had been mixed up, giving one user access to the profile of the other one.

Occurrences of these spontaneous information mix-ups will in my opinion be more or less inevitable within the large information systems handling billions of pieces of data around 2020. While I could say this will not be a problem because people will "pay closer attention" to avoid such things, unfortunately people also tend to say the same thing for road accidents. The best course of action is probably to supplement the secret-sensing capabilities of future software with the capacity to recognize other people's secrets and block access to them, while notifying the operator of the source application that a secret has been leaked.

We have already addressed the matter of mistakenly sent emails and content. Science has "advanced" to the stage that some email clients give warnings when we mention the word "attachment" in an email, but forget to append the actual attachment. We also get warnings if we forget to write a subject line. But two things remain unresolved: avoiding being misunderstood in written or spoken form, and preventing us from writing things we should not, such as secrets or other sensitive information. A psychological study published in 2005 and 2006 revealed that approximately 50% of electronic messages are misunderstood. We also performed poorly in terms of understanding the content shared with us: we estimate that we understand 78% of things, while the actual figure is no more than 56%. Meanwhile, we are much better at decoding spoken messages, with a mere 5% discrepancy between the estimated and actual ratio of understanding. Despite the fact that video and voice message sending capacities have skyrocketed over the past decade — just think of Snapchat videos and the endless supply of GIFs showing animals being dumb in adorable ways — the number of emails sent globally continues to rise. Their total volume is set to increase to 130-150 billion by the year 2017, meaning that there are 200 million chances every day to mess up something that we want to send or convey.

It would be worthwhile to consider adding features to the internal intelligence of email and chat systems, that could attempt to protect users from such errors, from revealing their secrets or communicating in unclear terms. The system could issue a warning along the lines of: "I do not recommend sending this sentence because it reveals that you have never been to New York, while you told the recipient in an email last year that you had just returned from a ceremony in New York, where you went to collect an award."

The system could rely on secret-sensing algorithms that would define an individual's risk based on her needs and the context, the potential for upset or embarrassment, using the risk evaluations described in previous chapters. This system would issue a warning or even prevent specific operations, thereby protecting the user's secrets or the user themselves from doing something rash and careless.

CHAPTER 17

THE NEVERENDING FUTURE

The dilemma of the transhuman wrapped in intimacy: should my secrets be seen by my neighbor or my computer?

The cybersecurity profession is still very undeveloped compared to the financial sector. This is why it lacks models, experiences and historical roots. This is why I cannot utter visionary words as my economist peers do, saying that the crisis is W-shaped or that the market is nervous, but the fall in the price of a barrel of oil will have a positive effect on the reproduction of bears in Schönbrunn zoo. We have a cyber secured cryptocurrency: Bitcoin, but we do not know who invented it. We have cyber bank robbers, but we do not know who they are. We have encrypted telephones, but we do not know what they hold. Billions of cybersecurity events are held every year, but we are unable to analyze all of them. There are cyber-bears on the Democrat Party's servers, but we do not know if they are Russian.

In other words, there are far more things that we do not know than those that we do, and this is reason for concern. I would love to say that we can just let it go and look into the future without any risk so that whatever I say, I've got no responsibility. However, this is unfortunately not true either, because technological progress has inevitably lobbied computers into every corner and every palm, and because we are surrounded by a cyberspace with labile security. We cyber security experts are expected to lead the way among such circumstances. But we are like industrial divers in the depths without torchlights.

There is one thing we know for certain about the future: humans will still remain a part of it for quite some time. I say "still" because since the emergence of more complex electronic machines and later, intelligent computers, i.e. the mid- and late-1990s, some theorists have put forward the advantages of combining humans and machines. Since then, futurism has taken on a more realistic form, referred to as transhumanism, meaning the development of human capacities using machines. This includes things like better hearing, sharper eyesight, lightning-quick memory, learning any foreign language, a stronger body and so on. Developing the human body has taken on the form of innovations such as the mind-controlled robotic arm developed by DARPA and worn by Johnny Matheny, a US citizen who lost one of his arms due to cancer in 2008, or the exoskeletons that enable handicapped human bodies to regain the capacity to move or allow a soldier to carry hundreds of pounds of equipment. So although we will still be here in the future as the human race, who knows in what shape or form? The changes will not be restricted to our physical bodies or certain capabilities, but also our minds, self-image and social habits. This must be taken into account when planning future security.

Current trends show that transparency is on the rise because it is impossible to keep such a quantity of things secret. So society has instead become more tolerant. We reveal more and feel less shame. This phenomenon was driven by the spread of cyberspace, and cyberspace constitutes its lifeblood. Facebook founder Mark Zuckerberg pinpointed this precisely, back in 2010: "People have really gotten comfortable not only with sharing more information and different kinds, but more openly and with more people... That social norm is just something that has evolved over time." His thoughts have been much criticized, leading to his withdrawal of them, but I have to agree with him and we have to believe his words, despite our reluctance to accept the idea. The public is growing in size and complexity; the question is how this affects intimacy. Will we have anything left that we can call private? With whom and how can we share this?

I have some good news for humanists: it is quite possible that intimacy will be humanity's refuge in an increasingly cyber-ized world. The personal connection between two people at a given moment in time is free of technology and may be the single way for us to retain some of our privacy in the future.

We can be certain that the level of intimacy will change, as recent years have shown how social media has transformed these levels. In a video of an air catastrophe in Dubai that was averted by a whisker in August 2016, we could almost watch live as the scared passengers and their family members ran down the landing strip, with a smoking and later smoldering 777 in the background, following an emergency landing due to a landing gear malfunction. Andy Warhol predicted 15 minutes of fame for everyone back in 1968, which not only became a reality with the emergence of the Internet, but now literally anyone, including the neighborhood butcher, can become a superstar. Since then, however, fame has begun to lose its significance. The New York Times published an article in 2008 about micro-fame, while the term 15-second nano-fame was coined in 2016. Everything has changed, with the efforts of secret service agencies and law enforcement bodies pitted against cyber criminal actions, while our own direct social environment is attacking our privacy from all sides. Today, it has become harder to keep ourselves secret than it was to become famous in the past.

Society has no choice but to adapt. Just like Zuckerberg said. The number of secrets and taboos is shrinking, while appetite for information and unusual needs are on the rise. In Iceland, there is an application that tells young people whether they are too similar genetically. Instead of leaving it up to chance to decide whether to take a fancy to somebody or not, I first check whether the other person's aunt is not my cousin.

Anybody who has ever visited a small town has surely experienced the suspicious gaze of some elderly local. A regular meme on cybersecurity websites is a picture of three elderly rural women sitting on a bench, strictly scanning their environment, with the inscription: "The perfect surveillance system." Horizontal surveillance has always played a role in the history of mankind. After all, it was the only option available until 200 years ago, right? People saw each other in villages. However, not all the information was available there either. Perhaps the priest knew what was going on in the neighboring diocese, but the average local did not. But if someone regularly disappeared at the same time that fruit went missing, they were likely to draw suspicion. There was no need for the more thoroughly informed priest, horizontal surveillance already existed.

Nobody had a problem with this just 200 years ago. Today, however, particularly in the wake of receding privacy, sensitivity has grown and social tolerance has decreased when it comes to surveillance. In a 2015 survey by the PEW institute, 93% of the US population considered it important to be able to know who receives information about them and to have power over controlling whom they share their personal information with. To put it simply: if somebody tells her best friend via an online chatroom that she has toenail fungus — which, by the way, affects a quarter of the total population and around half of the older population — she has no problem with the secret service listening in on the conversation, as long as nobody else finds out. Nobody wants others to know that she has toenail fungus.

We're talking about home treating a fungal disease, not about concocting ingredients to make a bomb. Remember? Although it is embarrassing, no harm will come from it. A classic white secret. This is why she never wears sandals in summer.

This shows how personal relationships become important in such situations, when two people are talking to each other, revealing their secrets and learning something about the other person. This is likely for multiple reasons: our awareness relaxes in such a situation, saves energy and does not have to focus on many things at once. The concept of friend and confidante are transformed and supplemented. We use these terms to refer to someone who we know will not record our words or movements with any technical tools, and will also be tolerant if we openly adjust wrinkled clothing, or scratch our stomach. He will not care if we stare into space, speak lazily or drink like a slob. These things mean that the relationship is considered truly safe, where the person feels more at ease than in the spaces ruled by cyberspace, which are likely to be basically everywhere by the year 2020. In this future, moments that are absent of machines, of the ever-vigilant cyberspace, of social media, will gain value, and will be coupled with the request: "Human implants off!" Interpersonality will be a particularly valuable thing. It will be intimate because it is safe. It is safe because it is intimate.

A secondary intimate zone is also likely to emerge. This will have meaning in the technological realm as well, because it seems unlikely that the only option for intimacy between people will be to meet in person. We are too comfortable and the world too fast-paced. A survey conducted in 2015 revealed that nearly 90% of American internet users over the age of 18 have already tried sexting, and people who are in relationships derive greater sexual pleasure from sexting than their single peers. Technological zones allowing intimacy and the exchange of secrets could come in the shape of secure virtual realities, some kind of 3D projectors with restricted access, or encrypted written, audio or image connections.

But these will have two preconditions. First, if they are not preceded by a personal meeting where the seed of intimacy is planted, they will have far less value for us. And secondly, a cyber security environment for communication where people's rights to privacy are fundamentally guaranteed.

The latter is a more difficult matter, but not unfeasible. We have just not yet found the "sure thing." In terms of protecting private secrets, most of society has believed the state, the secret service, the police, hackers, data leakers, hacktivists, freedom fighters; but the cyber coin seems to have 100 sides. Nearly everything has been revealed to be vulnerable, not good enough, not what it appears to be, never what it had appeared to be, interest-driven or an outright lie, and so on.

Of course there is always hope. In 2016, the world believes in people such as the rebel cybersecurity expert Moxie Marlinspike, a committed advocate of privacy, who invented Signal, the encryption software considered to be the safest in 2016. But who knows where Signal and Moxie will be in 2020 or later. Just as we do not know what happened to Truecrypt, which offered de facto and accessible encryption to anyone between 2004 until 2014. Or Netscape, which was the default browser of the past and later introduced SSL encryption, now nearing extinction. Where is WEP, the super security algorithm for Wi-Fi connections created in 1997? And its successors WPA and WPA2? The list is long. These were all solutions that were the Holy Grail of security once upon a time, but were revealed five or ten years later to having been freely accessed by secret service agencies or hackers. We do not know whether we can believe them or not. To cite the chief of security of a large bank, who has seen quite a lot in his time: "We just look on without knowing what to do, like a squirrel in a forest fire." In a nutshell, there is no guarantee that we will be able to achieve a level of security that modern society will fully trust, and name choices such as PGP, aka Pretty Good Privacy will not help (this is an encryption ecosystem that has remained true to its name to date).

It is well worth considering that in the future, not only are the structure of public and intimacy levels bound to change, but also the structure of trust. In the late 1990s, the security world was already reading the work of US IT security expert Marcus J. Ranum — also the creator of the first truly effective firewall — who spoke of the transitive trust that emerges when networks and machines trust each other. By the second half of the 2010s, transitive trust can be established between anything and anyone. When we log into a website and navigate onto another website owned by the same corporate group, for instance skype.com and microsoft.com, we are likely to retain our status and remain logged in on the latter website.

Citing comfort, users hand out their trust and have no qualms about using their Facebook or Google accounts to use third-party services, regularly checking the "Remain logged in" box when being identified, and providing thousands of access rights to remote drives. We hand over this same trust when using the service and checking the "I accept the terms & conditions" box below the legal disclaimer on data processing. My favorite was the Netflix website, which I was lucky enough to open on a smart television set. When I logged in, the system displayed a message that I was currently on page 1 out of 104, and prompted me to either read the entire thing or accept all of the terms and conditions. Which do you think I opted for?

The big data leak cases cause even the most optimistic users to question whether it is wise to blindly trust the services offered and cyberspace and their operators. In mid-2015, the infidelity website Ashley Madison was hacked and the details and names of people looking for an affair were revealed. This disclosure of more than 30 million user profiles caused tragic suicides and harassment, and wreaked havoc among numerous human relationships across the globe. In August 2016, a team of Ukrainian hackers infiltrated the Central Ohio Urology Group (COUG) and stole hundreds of gigabytes of medical data, including x-ray images and personal patient information.

Against this backdrop of distrust, the security industry has two options: it must either quickly come up with something, or allow users to take matters into their own hands. The latter option is not so far from reality as it seems at first glance. In December 2013, the pilot of a Boeing 737 suffered a heart attack when the plane was 30,000 feet in the air. While one of the passengers, a certified nurse, tried to resuscitate the pilot, another passenger, Mark Gongol, a US Airforce pilot, agreed to take over the plane at the request of the cabin crew. The plane was ultimately landed safely and the pilot survived the adventure. We must never underestimate people's capacity to resolve a difficult situation themselves.

If warranted by data protection issues, it is possible that people will take back the trust conferred upon state institutions and corporations, and move towards tribal solutions. It seems that Gartner's analysts have seriously considered this as a viable scenario. Their 2020 forecast is called "Neighborhood Watch." In the model, victims of cybersecurity incidents in the future will be individuals for the most part, and if states or companies fail to take sufficient action to protect citizens or users, home and tribal remedies will emerge. In October 2015, researchers from security firm Symantec discovered virtual malware that had infected 10,000 internet routers, but surprisingly, the malware, instead of taking control of the infected machines, simply shut down the routers with weak passwords and obsolete systems, and warned system administrators to change the passwords and update systems. The messages left in the software called on

NSA and FBI staff to follow the lead of Snowden. A week later, it was revealed that the helpful malware was created by a team of do-gooder hackers referred to as the White Team, which also gave the software away for free public use. In response to questions about his background, a hacker from the group, who remains anonymous to this day, said, "I am a (mostly) normal citizen – I am not a well-known security researcher, not an activist, am not paid for this by company or state, and I do this strictly in my free time."

So if that certain threshold is reached at some point in time — for instance, Snowden 3.0 reports in 2019 that there is a secret American-Russian pact in the context of which the two countries' secret services are continuously exchanging data about the cyberspace activities of their respective citizens, in exchange for organizing a joint cyber attack against China (*this is all fiction, needless to say*) then people may withdraw their trust and pass it on to others. As far as I'm concerned, I would not be surprised if a social movement called Children of Cyber (CoC) would orchestrate the intervention, accompanied by the following video: "We are the Children of Cyber! We want our Data back! Our Trust is no longer yours to exploit! Our Secrets are not yours to tell." We should consider this a probable scenario, and should not underestimate its power or potential impact — in the early 2000s, most people failed to take the concept of Anonymous seriously.

Unsurprisingly, many companies are striving to regain the compromised trust of their users and customers. This was one of the main reasons for Apple's stubborn stance against the

FBI. Apple's CEO Tim Cook wrote the following in a letter to customers in February 2016: "Customers expect Apple and other technology companies to do everything in our power to protect their personal information, and at Apple we are deeply committed to safeguarding their data. Compromising the security of our personal information can ultimately put our personal safety at risk. That is why encryption has become so important to all of us." In my interpretation, this means that customer trust in a rapidly changing economic environment like the technology industry and in the uncertain world of cyberspace, is one, if not the single most precious corporate treasure that companies must protect at the price of their existence if they want to maintain long-term profits.

I once had a conversation with the head of security of a large industrial company. He was a middle-aged executive wearing a light-colored suit, with a proud expression and a self-conscious look in his eyes. I asked him how many strongly protected, sensitive users they had. He leaned forward confidentially, lowered his voice and asked: "Can you keep a secret?" The security profession is based on trust, and the past two decades for me have been informed by this trait. I looked in his eyes and said: "Yes, of course." He smiled in agreement, leaned back in his chair, and simply said: "So do we."

So far, we have looked at the 75% of secrets that we will be unable to protect by the year 2020. Now let's address the remaining 25% that we must do our best to protect at all costs. And not just us as individuals, but also corporations and states, each with their own respective secrets.

Since we are currently unable to adequately identify either the 75% or the 25%, as attested to by the data protection projects that have a hard time making progress, we probably have to adopt a new mentality. We must switch from using terms like personal data, healthcare data or financial data, to identifying secrets constituted from any type of data. Once we have identified and evaluated them, we will able to link them to data and information. This will allow us to better distinguish which data is important — i.e. associated with valuable secrets — and which is merely part of the 75%. The information security profession, aka cybersecurity, or whatever contemporary term will be used in the future, will probably have the task and responsibility of creating more palatable and relatable security systems (i.e. ones that function on their own), and to help corporate executives, state leaders, or members of law enforcement identify which 25% to focus on.

This will not be an easy task. Corporate leaders will have to give up on protecting large volumes of corporate data, currently considered confidential. It is possible that employee salaries will no longer be kept secret. All this in the interest of protecting what is really critical, for instance companies' acquisition plans. At the state level, the road leading to Snowden is a long one, but when a Secret Service agency like the NSA has to issue its first transparency report in early 2016, we can assume that there are also government level secrets that will have to be aired out in the interest of transparency and accountability. This is real transparency that includes environmental protection issues, economic and educational data, contracts, and strategic plans in multiple areas. However, information on locations where oil will run out by 2050 will be part of the strictly confidential 25%.

If we assume that people can identify this 25% of secrets to be guarded at any cost, the question of the credibility of the underlying information will still be an issue. Australian cybersecurity expert Troy Hunt is the creator of "Have I Been Pwned?" which allows users to check whether their user data has been included in any data leak campaigns. After the Anonymous attack in which the data of 55 million voters was stolen from the Philippines' voting system, Hunt addressed the signs indicating that the breach had really taken place and that the data was actually leaked, in an in-depth article. A seasoned professional security expert offers a 14-page argument and a 20-page professional debate on the topic: this is how uncertain security is. Data is not always evidence in and of itself, because we do not necessarily know where it comes from, while the data itself often reveals little. In order to find out whether a breach has actually occurred, Hunt generally follows a method where he asks the nearly 370,000 users who have already registered on the website and searched in the database. In other words, he seeks information from potentially affected users living in all points of the world. If he receives adequate corroboration, he can then prove that something really happened.

I could ask readers who have been to New York to put up their hands, but this would be embarrassing for a reader sitting in Starbucks, and I would not see your hands go up, so it would be futile. But I could ask those who have never been to New York how they know about the city's existence. The answer is simple: I know because a lot of people have spoken about it, because I have seen the city on TV, someone in the family was born there, my cousin went to school there, so I have sufficient evidence from various credible sources, evidence that cannot be erased and which can be confirmed by any of the sources at any time. Something similar is needed in data protection as well. Blockchain technology, which is also the procedure backing the digital currency Bitcoin, promises something along these lines. You can record any event in a digital chain of events in a manner that it cannot be deleted, and store the chain at many points or organizations across the world. So when you ask a blockchain system whether New York really exists, it downloads a chain from Tokyo, Sydney, Washington, Moscow, and Cuba in a matter of seconds, each containing the same thing: New York's architectural log, from the beginning until now, including accurate dates and New York's geographical coordinates. The same information channels from all points of the world, and we know that the content cannot be forged or modified, because the links of the chain are built upon one another. We have our credible response: New York exists. We can also state its date of establishment and location with full certainty.

A bank transaction, a user recording within a system, the recording of a piece of healthcare information in a hospital database, the installments of a loan repaid by a debtor, are all items that can be stored in a blockchain-based system. It was announced in June 2016 that seven different banks around the world, including both commercial and national banks, have started testing blockchain solutions. They intend to use the technology to improve their own operations. A week before, Canadian and German financial institutions successfully executed wire transfers using blockchain technology. The funny thing in this concept is that such a system is so perfect that certain experts are loath to implement it in the trading of stock exchange instruments, an area governed today by machines, auditors, and intermediary companies. This is because the solution is so fast, accurate and credible that it would put an end to tips and chicanery, and leave several intermediary companies in a difficult position. Meanwhile, bank customers would benefit from having their wires completed in a matter of seconds, and stock exchange trading would also be more secure and quicker. However things turn out, the technology is impressive because it gives a firm answer to the question of credibility and non-repudiation, and can be applied in an infinite number of areas.

Imagine that someone sent you a friend request on Facebook, along with a direct message to confirm their request. Even if we are suspicious regarding the person's actual identity, today we tend to decide based on how attractive their profile picture is and whether they have spelled their name correctly. A blockchain system would instantly reveal whether the person's identification data is credible, relying on confirmations of an unforgeable data chain from multiple sources. The system would instantly identify users who regularly troll the internet, i.e. the notorious liars. It would also put an end to the era when "nobody can tell on the Internet that you are a dog." Of course there is a flip side to the matter: imagine if somebody was sick but does not want anybody to know about it. Perhaps they have changed gender, are hiding from a stalker or are trying to conceal their original identity from the public.

And what about states; how do they regain trust, and do they want to regain it at all? Governments generally strive to find solutions that avoid complex and costly technologies. The NSA had already designed an encryption microchip two decades ago that contained a backdoor, meaning that the encryption could be decrypted with the right know-how. The chip would have been incorporated into communication devices, but the market was hostile to the concept. The famous encryption procedure PGP came into being as a social and market response to this. Since the Snowden scandal, it has been revealed that secret service agencies have since found new routes, "convincing" major internet providers and telecommunications firms to collaborate with them in order to allow them to access the necessary data. The many cases of data theft and internal abuse shed light on the fact that today, neither secret service agencies nor the state have proven to be adequate keepers of the data that they obtained or were given.

States have come up against a new type of hurdle since 2010. Companies started insisting on their rights, and more importantly, on the rights of their customers, while rock-solid encryption technologies became accessible to citizens. The irony of the situation is that governments still use very few of the secure technologies available to protect the data entrusted to them. Meanwhile, however, the world is faced with global issues such as the transition of organized crime into cyberspace and the emergence of modern communication technologies adopted by terrorists.

Law enforcement, anti-terrorism, and secret services suddenly found themselves in *2010: Odyssey Two*, facing the dilemmas of engineer Curnow on his first space walk. He cannot remain more than 15 minutes in space exposed to the radiation. His helmet starts getting foggy, he can barely see. He is nauseous. He needs to throw up, but if he does, he will choke inside his helmet. He cannot close his eyes because he needs to work, but cannot breathe too deeply either because his oxygen supply is limited. What can we do when we cannot do anything?

The encryption cannot be decrypted, user data cannot be disclosed, people do not want to be subject to surveillance; while spies, terrorists, criminals and the cyber soldiers of hostile states disappear without trace after committing acts of terror, stealing tens of millions of dollars, gigabytes of data, and even having blackmailed users or corporations, threatening to encrypt their data. Members of counter-intelligence or the police have no other choice but to throw up their hands and ask: how can I do the job that I took my oath to? What should a US state do with 200 undecodable smart phones seized from criminals and hindering the progress of a case? This new situation is by far the most difficult we are now faced with, and calls for a new approach from states. Although I wouldn't necessarily call prohibiting encryption *a new approach*, it is something the US, France, and the UK are considering. Or should companies be required to weaken encryption or put backdoors into their products, as suggested by earlier attempts? Likewise, barring telecommunications services because somebody is caught performing encryption is also not the right response. These techniques worked like a charm in the past but do not seem like optimal solutions today. There are nearly 900 encryption products existing in 55 countries across the world, almost every smartphone and chat application employs encryption, and ISIS has even developed its own encryption solution.

President Obama recently declared that he would like to grant experts access to certain encrypted content in the event of suspected terrorism, that in a particular content could jeopardize people's lives if not accessed. The issue, however, is complex: a solution needs to be found to give access to specific things for a small group of people, and the president of the US expects the technology industry to come up with a solution. In addition, who will the small group include, who will select them, and who will they be accountable to?

One possible solution is to introduce artificial secret-recognizing tools or behavior analysis tools to support or fully assume the handling of secrets. These could take on the form of algorithms installed in mobile telephones, computers or other devices, capable of recognizing when something represents a security threat, for instance something that presents the threat of an act of terrorism by the user. If the algorithm detects something of this sort, it does not warn or report the perpetrator, but if the investigative authority comes to a point where it would like to access the suspect's system, it could seek out this *protector of the secret* for assistance. The software or artificial intelligence could provide a mobile telephone search order or system search warrant tied to a specific objective, authorizing the device to take action. This could prompt the device to release the suspicious information that it deems to be connected to the case.

The encryption was not decrypted by the manufacturer. The authority did not receive anything that was not related to the case. The user could not conceal his actions on purpose. Information was not transmitted until reasonable suspicion arose. Everything can be evidenced. Privacy is only affected in the slightest way. Nobody is surveying the other person continuously. Everybody can calm down.

It is conceivable that if the decisions of machines were involved in dealing with the issues that humanity cannot solve, it could cut through the Gordian knot and help preserve secrets, privacy, and social order.

CHAPTER 18

DEEP FUTURE
AND SENSOR WORLD

*From Thai chili beans
to all-encompassing convenience,
and self-protecting data*

A classic IT joke tells of a programmer who is sent by his wife to the grocery store to buy milk. She tells him to buy a gallon of milk, and if there are eggs, to buy a dozen. So the programmer comes back with 12 gallons of milk. Answering his wife's questioning look, the husband explains: "There were eggs..." This way of thinking follows precisely the algorithmic principle, and even characterizes robots and software. This is how the programmer got the request wrong, thinking that if there are eggs in the store (if this condition is met) he should buy 12 gallons of milk instead of one.

However, if we make good use of such conditionality in global cyberspace or even in the cyberspace of our own home, we can connect different events together, and make our machines respond to them in clever ways. This is made entertaining by a service creatively called "if this, then that," ifttt.com. On the website you can set up what should happen in one application if something happens in another. For example, you should receive an email if it rains tomorrow. If my favorite show is on TV, the lights should switch off in the kitchen.

Through this service you can enter into a world where machines rely on each other to make smart decisions according to various conditions. By 2030 it will be commonplace for such automated ecosystems to surround us. Coupled with the IoT (Internet of Things) numerous sensors, smart devices, and ordinary objects connected to cyberspace will send us information, and we may even be able to give them orders. Soon it will be completely natural for me, while standing in the kitchen, to decide to cook Thai chili beans even though, unfortunately I don't know how to prepare them; but once I say it out loud, the recipe will appear on the side of my refrigerator, which will even tell me that some ingredients, beans and certain spices, are missing. It will also tell me that I could buy them in a nearby shop, but it is only open until 6:30 pm, and it is now 6 pm. So I would be just in time because the computer has calculated that under current traffic conditions it will take 12 and a half minutes to get there if I leave now. I think this nice feature would excite most people. It holds out the promise that we could spend precious time on things we enjoy more, or that we could be more productive. Of course, some people will insist on exploring the Thai chili beans recipe by themselves and selecting the necessary ingredients one by one, or they simply love to roam the grocery store; but they will most likely welcome similar computer assistance when repairing the broken lavatory cistern.

To make this happen in the future, we will build systems to collect, analyze and, forward information from everywhere. I must admit that this thought gives many cybersecurity experts a start. In 2012 at the Black Hat Conference in Las Vegas, a hacker demonstrated that using a $50 device he can hack the card-pass door locks used in 4 million hotels with a single movement. A professor at the University of Michigan easily managed to gain access to the PIN code for the Samsung smart lock in May 2016 using a lock-pick malware app he developed. These locks do not require a key because – theoretically – they can only be opened with the owner's mobile device. There will be unforeseeable consequences if these systems with weak security, and the information gained from them, become connected.

Yet it seems very likely that we will do exactly that. By 2020 there will be about 27 billion devices in cyberspace, and they will all be in communication with each other. Unfortunately, confidentiality breaches, legal cases, and accidents are also coded into this huge amount of information and system complexity. I believe we may even lose control. The A380-1000 airplane model produced by Airbus, which will fly from 2020, will contain 10,000 sensors in each wing, while the entire aircraft will "produce" 7.5 terabytes of data in a day. This is despite the fact that it is still unclear whether the IT systems of our planes can really be hacked

– as claimed by cybersecurity professional Chris Roberts in 2015, to the FBI agents who detained him.

The question is what will happen if masses of personal data are released from thousands of IoT devices, or if cybercriminals can see not only into our online life but also into our homes, e.g. they will be able to learn about our secrets through any device. For instance, in the description of Samsung smart televisions with voice recognition it is stated that we should not say any personal or sensitive information in front of the TV because that will be transmitted to third parties.

Even those who produce the software programs don't necessarily trust them. In 2016 a selfie made by Facebook founder Mark Zuckerberg spread online, in which we could see in the background that he had taped both the camera and the microphone of his laptop. Will the leakage of home data become a big problem? Not right away. Is it a secret that today I'm cooking Thai chili beans for dinner? No. What is more, I might feasibly want to share this experience with others. Underlying dangers have been never been encouraging for making people try out new things or buy in bulk, i.e. software producers are not interested in frightening users in any way. If we really like the kitchen robot assistant that makes our everyday life easier with the Thai chili beans recipe, then we will shut our eyes to the fact that we might reveal a great deal of our personal secrets via a microphone connected to the Internet in our kitchen. A sort of collaborative filtering takes place, namely that people with common sense wait, then look around and see what others do, and how, and then act in the same way as the majority. If the neighbors get one of these, I can have one too.

As for the masses of data, it is worth mentioning another concern. In the whole of cyberspace – i.e. in the totality of IT devices – data is in an extremely exposed position. I know I won't be popular for making the following analogy, but at least I can try: in my opinion, data is like a slug after rain. With a vulnerable body, which is not even protected by the shell typical of its fellow species, it crawls on the ground seemingly without any purpose or protection. If somebody notices it, they usually pass it by, or flick it quickly into a bush or under a tree so that others don't step on it accidentally. Generally though, after two minutes, the slug will be back where it was, and sooner or later somebody or something will step on it, and the poor thing will be gone. The bush and the large leaves are to the slug what software, database managers, or operating systems are to data: places where it can hide. And that is where the problem occurs. Basically, there is nothing to protect it, it lacks self-defense. I once talked to the famous Hungarian designer Ernő Rubik, inventor of the Rubik's cube, about security. He said that in his opinion, the development of security very much resembles the evolution of living creatures. He claimed that security should develop together with systems and data, as turtles also grow with their shell.

This means that data today receives as much protection as provided by a given application, database manager, or other software. If data is removed from where it has been so far, it loses that protection. Just think about the website Pastebin: you can copy and share simple text formats here, hence its name.

Self-protecting data structure

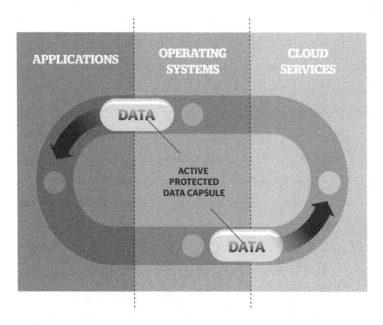

Although its operators have been expressly fighting against the publication of illegal content for years, most security companies still find many passwords, stolen, or leaked data here. This data "lived" for a while in a safe environment, in vain, because somebody at some point took it out of there and it can no longer protect itself.

That is how the idea of self-protecting data was born. To be precise, data would act like "live" and active applications, their home would be a sort of confidential capsule, and if anything or anyone, be it an application such as Facebook, or an operating system such as Windows, wanted to manage them, they could only do so if it did not involve removing them from their given environment. As if they were working with snails and their shells, instead of slugs. In this way data could determine by itself what protection it needed, it would no longer be vulnerable in its environment, and it would receive the same protection all the time.

Of course, there are some "minor" problems. To make this work, we would need to rewrite all of our existing IT systems from scratch, while our current memory and storage capacities would have to be substantially increased. And naturally, the question remains as to what would happen to the data that we keep in mind, take a picture of, or remove from its own protection in any other way. This would not be the first task in human history that seemed impossible, nor the most difficult, I think. The computer of the Apollo program's spacecraft in 1969 was simpler than the latest electronic razor, and had 1,000 times less memory than what is required in 2016 to catch a Pokémon. As JFK said in his famous speech, "We choose to go to the moon in this decade and do the other things, not because they are easy, but because they are hard..."

I have already presented this idea – without slugs – at a couple of conferences and events, and my colleagues did not start to throw used laptops at me right away. I believe we have to rebuild the foundations of our IT systems if we want to get a grip on data protection and thus on the problem of keeping secrets.

CHAPTER 19

I'M SORRY DAVE...

Epilogue, in which the two-meter tall,
120-year-old man no longer talks
to the machine, robots write poems
to one other, and, finally
a machine hand reaches out to us

In the cybersecurity profession, 2015-2016 is the period of Threat Intelligence. Although not every organization and vendor understands it in the same way, this essentially means that cybersecurity experts collect information from all the existing sources they have access to, e.g. dark web, Pastebin, hacker communities, and databases. They then analyze the results, looking for traces of possible data leaks or actual data, before handing over their conclusions to companies, countries, or anyone who can do something with them. This is in fact the intelligence activity of cybersecurity. Security company FireEye, for example, has several hundreds of security analysts working in cyberspace, but even the well-known RSA operates an Israeli center, which is specialized in cyber fraud prevention, employs more than a hundred experts, not to mention the other fifty or so tech companies that provide similar services.

But the time is drawing closer when this information will be returned to users through full-scale automations. Let's imagine that an employee receives an email in his account. This email will be analyzed by a complex system in terms of cybersecurity risks and confidentiality. Then it will inform the user that there is an 82.6% chance of it carrying some malware. It will even explain why: 38 minutes earlier, employees of two large oil industry corporations in the Middle East, along with three healthcare institutions in the US, received a letter with similar content. We do not know yet what it contains, but given that several groups linked to ISIS have referred to the above institutions as potential targets over the past three months, it recommends that the user should not open the email.

Stephen Hawking says we cannot restrict our use of machines. Humans are constantly building things without a break, and do everything for their own convenience and reproduction purposes. Only machines will be able to perform and produce automated responses similar to the above, recommendations suitable for human use, conjectures, and a quick analysis of opportunities and risks for humans. In order to preserve our secrets and security, we will create interconnected ecosystems providing security, which will seem to be convenient and useful at the same time. We will wake up in the morning at an optimal time advised by a machine or an application, and we will receive a recommendation from the same device as to what we should do during the day and in which order. Dr. Oliver Scott Curry, an evolutionary researcher at the University of Oxford, thinks that after a thousand years humans will be two meters tall and generally live for one hundred and twenty years, but the advantages and convenience provided by technology will come at a price, and after ten thousand years we may be a vulnerable species with weak immune systems. According to Stephen Wolfram, a British computer scientist and theoretical physicist, machines will operate in a completely different way to humans, and so we will have to learn how to talk with them, which will differ from how we talk to other people. This means we will have to adapt to each other. The question may arise as to how we will be able to make these big and complex computers understand what it means to us humans to be safe, why our private sphere is important to us – and what is it anyway? – and why we stick to intimacy, and our secrets.

If you have not yet met a bot, i.e. an automated machine that carries out human tasks, that is only because you have not noticed it. Maybe this book was also written by a machine? It's not impossible at all. In March 2016 a piece written by a novel-writing robot was successfully preselected at a short-story contest. Out of 1,450 contest pieces, eleven were robot-human co-productions. The younger brothers of such robots, the bots, have arrived in our life and are not only hunting on our behalf for products to be sold on the Internet, they also actively interact with users: they purchase and politicize. But what are they? Intelligent solutions

– typically software and applications – that carry out automated tasks, and simplify certain work processes or tasks. According to analysts' estimates, in 2016 this industrial sector may reach $9,000 billion, involve 230 million salaried workers, and even generate up to 800% profit. Those who are the least bit sensitive to economic realities will probably agree with me: "Bots will be wherever they can be." This evolution has already started. Today even people with an insider's eye cannot necessarily spot the bots among real humans. An acquaintance of ours rented a car in the US, and even talked to the unknown administrator on the phone for a while about what it is like to live in Europe. He was amazed how informed Californian people are about Europe, yet his chat partner was none other than a bot trained for this job. It had no opinion, but was familiar with things, it was effective and left a positive impression.

Newer evolutions of such robots will really raise the bar for the cybersecurity field, since new robots will be able to learn, copy and finally replace their owners. They will speak in their owner's human voice, imitating its style, accentuation and phrasing. In a telephone or online audio conversation it will be impossible to differentiate between the robot and the human. According to American geneticist and molecular engineer Dr. George Church, implanting our brain and thoughts in another entity – even a machine – will be a serious challenge, but one thing is for sure, if we are replaced by a machine that is basically a partial or full copy of our knowledge, we will still have to prove how identical it is to the original – i.e. to us – how authentic the copy is, and whether it is faulty or not. Do you still remember the small red recording light of dictaphones? The fear is that such robots will no longer have a red light.

But let's look on the bright side. With the use of such developed software, the time may come when my telephone, communicator, virtual glasses, or anything else I am going to use in the future *will recognize me*, know who I am, what I am doing, how I am thinking, and I will not mind if it is even partially myself. Today our personal IT tools live together with us, they know our pulses, forward our emails, oversee all of our browsing on the Internet, listen to all of our telephone conversations, and also see the selfies we take. Yet they do not know us, they do not know who we are. At the cybersecurity level I think that a modern security system should look out for my secrets instead of constantly asking me in which folder I keep the data I deem sensitive. It should rather understand what I am doing, who my family members and friends are, how I live, i.e. who I really am. Based on this it could make decisions for the benefit of my protection.

What will it be like to live in a world where most secrets are revealed within days and hours? People will know about many, many things. The age of major misunderstandings is coming, because although people may know everything, they will understand increasingly less from it. An authority, country, media or even hacktivists, people of cyberspace, can only react to this by starting to explain to people what needs to be understood. Who will be the interpreter? Whose role and power will be strengthened?

We do not know this yet, but there are already some things we perfectly understand. Data can be obtained, cyberspace transcends beyond all borders. In the middle of 2016, Estonia decided to store copies of important governmental data in the UK due to fears of Russian hackers. As the Estonian cyber leader puts it: "We need to be sure that whatever happens to our territory in the future, Estonia can survive." In the future, companies, organizations, and governments that work with their data in a smarter way, protect it better and search it more effectively, will be more successful. Everybody will have less control over their data and will have increasingly more secrets to keep. It may even happen that after a while we will have to hide them away from machines because they will be able to smell them. For example we will whisper them to a wax cylinder, which we will put into a box firmly sealed with a physical padlock.

In order to somehow find the balance between security and functionality, between the big open networks of the future and the private sphere, and between private secrets and law enforcement, IT experts will have to develop processes offering appropriate guarantees that everyone can access as much of the data stored in cyberspace as is justified. Here, unfortunately, they cannot only listen to state and government representatives, secret service agencies, legal aid organizations, hacktivists, freedom fighters, the press, or technologists. All of these say different things, and although they are all true to some extent, everybody has their own agenda as well.

There is no general truth. Let me quote the famous Hungarian writer and poet Frigyes Karinthy: "Everything is different." We cannot create a situation in which somebody wins because we will not allow ourselves to let anybody lose. The situation is complex and exciting, and for the first time in our history it may be that machines will help us to resolve the human dilemmas that we can no longer solve among ourselves.

CHAPTER 20

THE "NO" CLOUD

At the end of one of my university lectures on cybersecurity, I asked the students if they had any questions. There was an awkward silence for a while, before a female student said: "Is there anything that you *are* allowed to do in cyberspace?" I would gladly have said to her: "No." Then I imagined the parties, photos, adventures, excitement, love, and experiences that they would miss out on if they genuinely did nothing with their mobile phones and Instagram, and I tried to come up with a few innocent tips. I have to admit, it wasn't easy. I struggled for a while, then gave up. "Impossible," I said to myself. While I was collecting information with my colleague Zsuzsa Szvetelszky during the writing of this book, I remembered those university lectures. This gave rise to the "wall of impossibility," on which I wrote all of the things that we shouldn't do if we want to be safe in cyberspace. It is alarming as a whole, but it does make sense if taken one-by-one. Let's take a look...

The wall of impossibility...

Researchers of the future always say we should start from the past when we want to see the future. We can't take something into account that has yet to be invented. The joint future of cybersecurity and society nevertheless takes us down paths where we have to look far ahead. Will machines or people guard our secrets in the future? Who will be at the controls? It's not great news I'm afraid...

CHAPTER 21

TOOCHEE – A BAD DAY

Philip Noret and Michael Rose, agents of the FBI's domestic counter terrorism unit, left their cars just around the corner and started to stroll down the street towards the south. An old truck stood at the end of the road, two hundred meters away, the kind road construction workers like to take a rest in. But this truck had no signs on its sides and its windows were black. The two agents stepped towards the truck and knocked on the door. It opened, and the two men got in.

The truck was actually electronic surveillance HQ no. 17 of the New York branch of the FBI. The loading area was filled with computers, communication and surveillance devices. Three people sat in front of the monitors. Mitch Dockers, the lead agent, sat on the nearest chair. Noret and Rose had known each other for a long time, working together on several cases.

– Hey Mitch.

– Phil! Mike! Hey there. What brings you here?

– Pole and Stilton had an accident an hour ago.

– What? No! Are they okay?

– Both of them are in hospital. It's not too bad, but they won't be fit to work for weeks. The car was self-driving, but somebody else was at the wheel. He couldn't react quickly enough to the situation. We took the case.

– Okay, – said Dockers.

– Mitch, you look pretty beat, – said Rose.

– Yeah, tell me about it. What goes around, comes around. My home system was hacked.

– You're kidding me. Yours? I don't know anyone as precise, strict and paranoid as you when it comes to security.

– The weakest link. My kid downloaded some free program and they got in that way.

– Man, is the damage serious? – asked Noret.

– So far it seems it's not. They probably just wanted to have some fun. They reprogrammed the house. When I got home I found the communication system having a conversation in a style that would have gotten it thrown out of the worst pub. The refrigerator talks to me like an unassuming prostitute, I can only listen to thrash metal on my Hi-Fi system, and they subscribed to a bunch of porn channels. Oh yeah, and they sent 50 pizzas to the homeless shelter. Fortunately, the shop took back the box of Dom Pérignon champagne. But I'm going through everything now to see if they did anything serious in the background.

– That's tough.

– Yeah but I was still lucky. But now let's work. What do you know about the case?

– Only what we saw in the file, – said Noret.

– That's not much. – Dockers shook his head. – But there's not much more.

The man in his forties, who was already going gray, dug into his scarce hair as if wondering where to start. Dockers pointed to a folder on his own monitor and flicked it away with a quick motion. The folder flipped onto the central monitor and its contents were scattered on the virtual desktop. Dockers pulled a few receipts and bank statements to the middle.

– The system monitoring purchases, money movements and banking transactions came up with this name with the suspicion of domestic terrorism. Headquarters checked it out and found the suspicion to be justified. They ordered surveillance. It's been going on for 53 hours and 21 minutes. – Dockers looked at the counter on the wall. Here's the surveillance permit and the judicial permit for the electronic house search.

– The guy is Adam East, a 39-year-old sales manager, – said Dockers as he pulled another folder onto the monitor. He's made some interesting purchases in the past month. He's not a farmer-type guy, yet he bought a significant amount of fertilizer in seven stores in two states. And some little things, – added Dockers pointing to some receipts. – After this, we checked the purchases made by his wife too. We also found some interesting things. – The agent showed new invoices.

– What have you come up with so far? - Noret asked.

– We launched some data mining: the SWEET-L, SKY and SUE systems. SWEET-L searches for the person in social media and builds up his entire virtual personality from available data.

In the same place, SKY maps his social network, searches for problematic relationships, friends and hazardous hubs. SUE searches for information on other parts of the Internet, while Dirty SUE endeavors to track him down on the Dark Net.

– And what about GovNET?

After spying, virus attacks and hacking became too big a problem, while preventing and combating them as well as the vast damages still occurring, put an unbearable burden on those hacked, a network system was developed independent of the Internet, at significant cost, with the involvement of public institutions and the military, the financial sector and large industrial companies. GovNET became like the Internet used to be when it was launched: a closed elitist world.

– That's the basis, we're checking that first.

– Any results?

– Nothing special or out-of-the-ordinary unfortunately. So far they seem to be average in all respects.

– Political background? What about their past? – asked Rose.

– Practically nothing for East. We haven't even found anything from his university. Not even a demonstration or a political group. The apolitical generation of the twenty-first century. He didn't even register to vote.

– Apolitical? – Noret scratched his chin. – No, this is too sterile for my liking. There is no such thing as a totally apolitical person. At least during tax return filing time he surely criticizes the government. Or in a shop at the cash desk. While they're young, everybody is a revolutionary unless they were born into a rich family.

– Well. – Dockers spread his arms – We have been going through the guy's past for two days now, and we haven't found anything.

– Or maybe he hides it too well, – said Rose.

– Possibly. – Dockers nodded. – But there's no sign of it.

– His wife is a different case. Eleanor Dickinson came from a suburban blue collar family, she received a scholarship for university. She was actively involved in politics at university, she's a member of the Democratic Party, but she has some strong left-wing sentiments. She met East after university. They got married after two years. During that time she gave up on politics, at least, we've not found any trace of such activity. She worked and then had children.

– Relationships? - Noret asked.

– There are a few strange things here. When she took her husband's name upon marrying him, she changed her first name to Nora. This is how Eleanor Dickinson became Nora East. After graduating from university it seems as if she turned away from her past. She is not in touch with either her high school or her university. She hasn't attended any reunions. There is no trace on social media of her keeping in touch with anybody from those days. Her name or photo does not show up on the profiles of any of her former friends, groups or classmates. Her public life on social media is very limited. She hardly shares any personal stuff. As if she has isolated herself from the world.

– Anything else?

– So far, nothing. – Dockers spread his arms.

– What are you monitoring now?

– East's home. On paper, it's an average family. Dad, mum and two kids. The parents are working, the two kids (boys, 15 and 9 years old) go to a school nearby. The elder brother comes home alone, while the younger stays at school for the afternoon, their neighbor brings him home together with his own kids, every day. A typical suburban family. Maybe even too average.

– What did you find out here?

– Not too much. It seems this is the real situation. They definitely live there and the house is not a hiding place for a sleeper cell. Look, here is the info we obtained. We managed to get access to all the important systems. We checked all the smart meters. These showed that the consumption of electricity was very low during the past two days between 9 a.m. and 3 p.m. More or less what the refrigerator and some devices consume on standby. Even the water meter can be read in remote mode, and according to that, there was no water consumption. They have an alarm which is connected to a remote surveillance company. We asked there too. The alarm system was switched on at the given time, it was not switched off even for a minute, and the motion detectors did not signal anything either. So during this time, the house was empty. The surveillance cameras did not signal any movement that would contradict the residential records. Everybody is either at work or at school. Nobody can hide there.

That's not all, – said Dockers – get a load of this. Since pumas sometimes wander into the area from the forest, surveillance drones monitor the area, with infrared lights, and they search for signs of extra carbon dioxide emission. But even this system signaled nothing.

– Well, – Rose said – This really isn't a terrorist base.

– No, it isn't. – Dockers shook his head.

– Is it a house or an apartment? – asked Noret.

– A house. Here's the floor plan. – Dockers pulled the drawing onto the monitor right away. – Two floors, a double garage, kitchen-dining room-living room downstairs, four rooms and a bathroom upstairs. The two on the left side belong to the kids, the parents' bedroom and the study are on the right.

– How do you know this? – asked Rose. – It's not on the floor plan.

Dockers smiled.

– Internet traffic. Cartoon channels in No. 1 on the left, until 9 p.m. at the latest. YouTube and Facebook traffic in No. 2 on the left. Until 1 a.m.

– And which is the parents' bedroom?

– No. 1 on the right. The television and the Internet are connected to that. Only Internet in the other room. That's the study.

– Data traffic? Messages, mails?

– Unfortunately nothing. Everything is encrypted. We don't see anything of it.

– Anything else?

– Nothing. – Dockers shook his head. – If I monitored my mother, we would find more.

– So what now? – Rose asked his colleague.

– We won't get anywhere this way – Noret said, thoughtfully. – Let's have a chat with them.

– Terror threat protocol? Should a S.W.A.T. unit arrest them? – asked Dockers.

Nora East parked her car in front of the garage. She pulled her bags out of the trunk. As she left the car, it locked itself automatically. Of course, the bicycle of her younger son, Jake, was lying on the lawn near the garage. She propped it up against the wall. A red light flashed on the motion-detecting camera above the entrance. The door opened.

– Hi Nora, welcome home, – said the house's operating and communication system in the voice of George Clooney, whom they nevertheless called Fester. When they moved in this was the name of the pre-programmed voice, taken from a character in *The Addams Family,* and although they had replaced it several times, the name remained. But for a behavior pattern, they used the style of a butler.

– Hi, Fester. Is anybody home?

– Jake arrived half an hour ago.

– Jake! – shouted Nora.

– Hi, Mum! – shouted Jake from upstairs.

– Hi! Bicycle! Would you put it into the garage?

– I'm going over to Jimmy's later.

– Still, put it away, please! If it gets stolen, you won't get a new one!

– All right. I'm coming.

A nine-year-old boy ran down the stairs and went to the entrance.

– Stop! – his mother said.

Jake stopped.

– Any kiss for mom?

Jake jumped on her, kissed her cheeks and then ran out of the door. He jumped onto his bicycle.

– I'm going on a ride! – and before his mom could say anything, he had sped off and disappeared. Nora just waved.

– Fester! – she said as she was putting down her bags. – Close the door, please!

– Ok! – Fester said, and the door closed.

– Fester! Has anything happened at home?

– Nothing of note.

Nora shook off her high heels and sat on the couch.

– I'm hungry and tired. Would you make a quick sandwich for me, please? My favorite.

– Salami-cheese-mayonnaise?

– Yes.

– Unfortunately, I can't.

– Why? Is something missing?

– Of course not. Everything is available in the refrigerator. However, the lab results from this morning are problematic.

– Did you smell my pee again? – Nora asked, bitingly.

– Of course, I performed the usual daily tests.

– And what did you smell now?

– There is no problem with your urine, its specific weight is a little higher than usual, so I recommend that you drink a glass of water before you go to bed. The problem is with your weight.

Nora gulped, and said nothing.

– As you can see for yourself, – Fester continued in an emotionless voice. – You have exceeded your average weight by three kilos. Your doctor recommends a diet.

– So you already warned my doctor! You snooper! – Nora retorted. She hated the thought that even her weight could no longer be kept secret.

– I did not have to warn him, the data is automatically forwarded to your patient records. Among other things this is also a precondition for your cheaper health insurance. But I have to remind you that if your excess weight rises above five kilograms, your insurance premium will rise.

– All right, dictator. I don't want the sandwich then. I'm gonna take a shower.

Nora stood up and started to walk up the stairs.

– Nora, you asked me this morning to remind you that you want to replace my voice sample. Do you have any specific requests?

Nora stopped on the stairs.

– Adolf Hitler? – she suggested, in a slightly irritated voice.

– I'm sorry, he's on the list of banned persons.

– That's a pity, since it suits you very well at the moment. Kim Jong-un?

– Also prohibited.

– I've got it! you, J. Edgar Hoover!

– The founder of the FBI is allowed. There is a voice sample for him, I'll download it right away...

– For Pete's sake! Please don't! – Nora interrupted. – That's all we need just now. Remind me again at the weekend.

– OK. I will remind you when you're in a better mood.

– Good. If you take away my sandwich, don't try to ask me for anything.

Half an hour later, Nora walked downstairs, refreshed after a hot shower and changed into new clothes. She went into the kitchen and sat on a chair.

– Fester, any mails today?

– A few notices, some newsletters, promotions.

– Give me the letters, please.

The kitchen table turned into a monitor. The table was divided into two: on the left was open content available for everybody, such as music, photo albums, family videos, movies, holiday plans, calendar, shopping lists and reminders. Nora's private stuff, correspondence, calendar and other personal files appeared on the right. Although this part was encrypted, the program was able to identify Nora clearly from her movements, gestures and voice, so there was no need for a PIN number or code word.

– Fester, I'm hungry. What can you put together for me quickly that is healthy?

– One moment, please. Based on the stock of the refrigerator, I can recommend 11 types of sandwich and salad. In light of your tastes, I recommend toast with avocado and tomato, with some feta cheese.

– All right.

Nora already knew that in many respects, Fester knew her much better than she did herself. It had been observing her habits, tastes and even her mood from the first moment they moved in. Nora could have stood in front of the refrigerator and, after two or three minutes of searching and deliberation, and an argument with Fester, she would more or less have come to the same conclusion. Fester made the decision for her in one millionth of a second, and she did not have to face the fact standing in front of the refrigerator that she cannot eat a lot of the things inside it.

Two long, triple-jointed robotic arms came rolling on a track and stretched out from under the kitchen table. One of them opened the bread basket, took a slice of bread, put it into the toaster and switched on the device. It reached out to the shelf, grabbed a cutting board and took a plate out of the cupboard.

The other arm silently slid to the refrigerator and opened the door. It pulled open the vegetable drawer and put a tomato followed by an avocado onto the cutting board. With a swift movement it reached to the back of the upper shelf and took out the cheese box, without touching anything else, and closed the door. All of this took just a few seconds.

The two arms met in the middle at the cutting board, one of them carefully holding the tomato, while the other pulled out a chef's knife. It quickly cut four slices to a width of exactly four millimeters. It peeled the avocado and cut as many slices as were needed to cover the toast.

When the toast was ready, an arm took it out, spread cheese

evenly over it, in two to three quick movements, layered the vegetables on top, placed it on a plate, and put it in front of Nora.

The arm grabbed a small transparent box from the cupboard, swiftly drew barcodes on its cover, then put the vegetables in it and placed it in the fridge. It put all the tools into the dishwasher, before folding its arms back into the cupboard.

While the sandwich was being prepared, Nora was checking her correspondence. Each family member had their own private email address, but the house itself had one also. Invoices, bank statements and official governmental correspondence were all received at this address, along with mail related to the property and the family, as well as invitations. And naturally, a lot of advertisements.

Three tax letters and three insurance letters were at the top of the list. They were sent to her husband, to her elder son, Sly, and herself. She immediately knew that the first three were about the monthly road tax. Since black boxes had been installed into cars, not only was it easier to investigate accidents, but driving habits had also changed drastically.

The government had canceled highway fees and other road charges. In their place, they had introduced the monthly road toll. You pay for every road that you use, and the amount depends on the quality of the road. The expressway is the most expensive, while smaller sideroads are the cheapest. But you have to pay for everything, depending on the miles you drive in a given month. The black box sends the GPS data to the tax authority at the end of each month. Everybody knows exactly how much they have driven, on what types of roads. Although the government promised that this system would be more favorable, the majority of people are still paying more than before.

She picked up the sandwich and took a bite. It was better than she had expected and so she was happy to take another bite. In the meantime, she looked at the other three letters. *Vehicle insurance.* The insurer gives a discount if they have access to the data of the black box. Without this, the owner could find himself in the highest premium band and have to pay a fortune. But based on the data, they assess driving habits and insurance risks and give a customized proposal. It was worth passing on the data because calm, safe drivers received huge discounts from their premium. Those using self-driving cars receive the highest discounts. Additionally, the insurance is not tied to a vehicle but to a specific person, so you can borrow someone else's car.

Nora has a higher rating than her husband because she is a slower, calmer driver. Yet her husband pays less. The new insurance system does not have a lump sum premium but works on a pro rata basis, if you drive less, you pay less. Two years ago, when Nora broke her leg and had to stay at home for two months, the invoices had zero amounts on them. That is why the premium is lower for her husband. As a sales manager, he drives a company car. The kilometers allowed for the company car are invoiced to the company. Adam only has to pay for the few kilometers he drives during the weekend.

The door opened, Jake ran in and Sly entered at the same time. He is 15 but he is already six foot two and his feet are a size 12.

– Mum, I'm home! – shouted Jake.

– Hi, Mum! – Sly greeted her as well. He threw down his things, went to his mother and kissed her. He tried to steal the sandwich but his hand hesitated in mid air.

– Yuck! What's this? – Sly looked at it with feigned disgust.

– My afternoon snack. Healthy.

– It sure is, – Sly agreed. – It's yours.

He picked up the stuff he had thrown down next to the door and started to go upstairs.

– Sly! – cried his mother. – Come back!

Sly turned back unwillingly.

– Yes?

– Come here!

– Sly went back to the kitchen.

– What? – he asked, sounding bored.

– This is for you.

– What's this?

– Insurance invoice.

– Haven't you heard of the privacy of letters?

– Don't be cheeky! When I don't have to pay for your insurance, then you can speak up!

– So what? – the boy shrugged his shoulders.

– The premium is higher than usual.

– I probably rode my bike more.

– No, my dear son! – Nora said. – It's written here. They increased your premium because of your driving habits.

– So what?

– What do you mean "so what"? Are you getting wild with your bike? Do you ride too fast?

– No, not at all. But let me go, I have to study.

– We'll come back to this when your dad gets home.

Sly shrugged his shoulders defiantly and quickly ran upstairs.

– Fester, would you download the holiday pictures from my computer? Group them as usual and label them. Upload them to the family photo album. And send a notification to my parents.

– Okay, – Fester said.

Nora opened her mail. She ran through the latest correspondence but found nothing of interest.

– Nora, there is a problem.

– Yes?

– The pictures. I recommend that we do not upload all of them to the family photos.

– Why?

– The photos taken on 21 September after 11 p.m.

– Gosh! – Nora held her hands in front of her mouth.

– May I recommend we put them in your private folder, encrypted? Giving access to Adam?

– Yes, thank you, Fester.

On that day, Nora and Adam had let loose a little more in the holiday atmosphere and drank a little too much. And the evening wind was so stuffy. Emotions ran high in their room and some photos were taken. She would feel really small if her mother or mother-in-law saw them.

Outside, a yellow, box-shaped drone slid beneath the

window. It rolled in front of a gray door and turned towards it. A bar code appeared on the drone's monitor and it sent its identifier electronically. Fester recognized the code. The department store nearby sent this confirmation receipt for ordered products.

The gray door, which actually opened from two sides, was a cooler protected by an electronic lock. The drone also opened its door, and rolled the order that was wrapped up in a rolling box into the cooler. The drone locked its own door and waited until the cooler was safely locked as well. The drone registered the delivery as complete and returned immediately to the department store.

– Nora, the ordered goods have arrived, – said Fester.

– Take them out, please.

It would have been enough just to give orders, there was no need for politeness. But Nora, like most people, immediately endows a personality upon the object with which they communicate. Fester was not artificial intelligence but rather a family friend. She could not help but be polite with it.

The two robotic arms appeared from the cupboard again. A quiet beep was heard from below the window and a green LED lit up above the gray cupboard. The two doors of the cooler were protected by an electronic lock so that its contents could not be stolen. The internal door could only be opened if the external one was closed. This type of locking process prevented wandering animals or strangers from getting in through the box.

The internal door opened and the robotic arm rolled the box to the refrigerator. The two arms quickly took out the food and placed them on the shelves in the crossfire of cameras and scanning infrared lasers. Fester not only knew where each package belonged, but he also read the label codes and knew exactly which package contained what, what their weight was and when they would expire. So nothing would be forgotten at the back of the fridge, and nothing could expire. He put the hygiene products into a small basket and placed them onto a table next to the door. Nora would take them up to the bathroom.

– Nora, – said Fester. – There is a small problem.

– What's up? – asked Nora without looking up from her correspondence.

– The frozen stuff does not fit into the freezer.

– What frozen stuff?

– 11 kilos of ice cream.

– What? – Nora looked up, flabbergasted.

– 11 kilos of ice cream.

– I didn't order any ice cream.

– It was on the order list, I ordered it and it was delivered.

– Who added it to the list?

– It was recorded at 2.37 p.m. Only Jake was at home at that time.

– Jake! – Nora's voice nearly pierced through the house. – Come down right away!

Jake ran downstairs in a few moments.

– Yes, mom?

– What did you order from the shop?

– Me? – the boy asked. – Nothing.

– Yesterday afternoon. – Nora's voice was ominous.

– Nothing. Really.

– And the ice cream?

– What kind of ice cream? – Jake asked, more quietly.

– Yesterday afternoon someone ordered ice cream and only you were home.

– Not only me, – Jake protested immediately. – Jimmy was here too. We pretended to be spacemen. The table was the steering station, while the fridge belonged to the armory officer.

– And?

– Jimmy and I were playing. That's all. We only pushed the panel.

– But Jimmy cannot push the panel. He's not a family member.

– Well, no. I told him the code. Then he was able to push it.

– What? You gave away the code?

– No. – Jake sounded scared now. – I only told him. We were playing. Astronauts.

– Jake, what did I say to you about the codes? Entrance door, bicycle lock, Fester's code. What did I say? That you mustn't share them with anybody. This is a secret.

– But I didn't reveal it. We were just playing.

– I told you that you mustn't share it with anybody. Nobody outside the family!

– But Jimmy's not a stranger, – Jake said, his mouth drooping. – He's my friend.

– But he's not a family member. You shared it with Jimmy, who ordered 11 kilos of ice cream.

– That's good! – Jake's face lit up. – Now we will have plenty.

– But we won't. Because we don't want it, it is too much. Because it doesn't fit into the freezer. You cannot send frozen stuff back to the shop.

– So we have to eat it all today? – asked Jake in a hopeful voice.

– No, we won't eat it. What's more, I'm going to deduct the price from your pocket money. And we won't buy the toy I promised you. Now go to your room!

Jake ran upstairs, almost crying.

Nora pulled her hair back. – Fester! How much can we fit in the freezer?

– Four boxes.

– Good. Put together a dinner menu that requires the most frozen raw materials. It shouldn't be too lavish, just everyday food. And, if possible, everybody should like it.

– As soup I recommend Brussels sprout cream soup with potato dumplings. We have one and a half bags of frozen Brussels sprouts. Let's put frozen gnocchi into it as potato dumplings.

– Great idea! Go on!

– Sirloin rolls with mushroom and mixed vegetable pie.

– I don't know this recipe.

– I improved on Beef Wellington a little. We'll cut the sirloin into big slices, heap some seasoned mushrooms on it, and roll it up. As a garnish, the pie will be made of puff pastry, we'll stuff it with mixed vegetables. The sirloin, the forest mushroom mix, the veggie mix, and the puff pastry are all in the freezer.

– You're a god, Fester! How many boxes will be left this way?

– This way only three boxes will be left out. And, – Fester seemed to hesitate for a moment. – I recommend ice cream for dessert.

– Haha, very funny. So we don't have enough space for two boxes?

– No.

– OK. I'll take it to the neighbors, and ask them to store it for us for a few days. Or they could even buy it from us.

– Great idea!

– Fester!

– Yes, Nora!

– Emergency situation. I'll continue the diet from tomorrow.

– That is understandable.

– Start cooking now. I'll run over to the neighbor with the two boxes.

Nora picked up the ice cream and ran out of the door with them. The two robotic arms started to carefully rearrange the freezer.

The front door opened half an hour later and Adam East stepped in.

– Hi, honey! – Adam shouted towards the kitchen.

– Hi! – Nora said.

The man in his forties put down his bag, coat and jacket.

– Kids?

– In their room.

Adam loosened his tie, went into the kitchen and kissed Nora. He looked around.

– Wow! What a spread! – Adam halted. – Are we celebrating something? Have I forgotten something?

– No, you haven't forgotten anything. We're celebrating that Jake ordered 11 kilos of ice cream and I had to empty the freezer.

– What?

– Forget it, I'll tell you later.

– All right. – Adam let it drop. Many years together had taught him when he should leave things in his wife's hands.

Nora threw off the apron and washed her hands. The robotic arm sprang forth and put the apron in its place, then quickly cleaned the counter.

– The main thing is, – Nora said, as she sat down. – That dinner is being prepared. And it'll be delicious.

– That's enough for me.

Adam took out a can of beer, and the refrigerator automatically registered that the stock had decreased by one can. A new order needed to be placed soon. Adam sat down by his wife.

– Any news?

– We received some bills: road tax, insurance.

– Adam pulled his messages in front of him and opened them with a tap. He started to read.

Suddenly, a yellow warning sign appeared before him.

– What's that? – asked Nora.

– Oh, I completely forgot about it. It's an invitation to Phil Ingram's weekend party. The mail program signaled that I have to respond.

– Did you ask for a reminder?

– No. – Adam shook his head. – I completely forgot about it. I read it and wanted to respond but it went out of my mind.

– So where's the warning from?

– This is my new mailing system. It interprets the contents of letters and processes them in advance. It puts advertisements into a separate place. It recognizes official and private mails, and indicates if I have to respond to anything. They wanted a response by tonight, and I haven't responded yet so it warned me.

– Shall we go? - Nora asked.

– No, he always invites his brother-in-law – he's a jerk. I can't stand him. - Adam grimaced. - Mailing program! – he said. – Response template, polite decline. The reason is that I will be at a conference.

A red message appeared on the screen.

– The calendar does not contain any programs for that day. Should I register the conference? Nora laughed. – Well, it won't let you lie.

– Mailing program! – said Adam. – Response template, polite rejection. The reason is that my dad died and we have to arrange the inheritance issues.

– But your dad died half a year ago...

– So what?

Another red message appeared on the screen.

– What's that? – Nora laughed again. – Is your mom busy too?

– No. – said Adam, suddenly serious. – It warned me that after the death of my dad, I sent out a circular to my friends about his death and I already rejected the invitation to the summer party for the same reason.

– Honey, the program seems to be smarter than you. You would have discredited yourself badly if you had sent that.

– I would have had to explain myself endlessly. – Adam scratched his ears. – Mailing program! The reason is because of other family programs.

The text of the letter showed up in a tenth of a second. Adam ran through it.

– OK. Send it!

Nora lifted her head. – Oh, I almost forgot it. We received this. – She put Jake's insurance in front of Adam. – The young man is getting wilder, his insurance premium has been raised. You'll have to talk to him this evening. I don't want to see him on a stretcher.

– Neither do I. I'll talk to him. – Adam started reading the insurer's notification.

– Adam! – said Nora in a sharp voice. – What's this?

– What?

– This, – said Nora pointing to a line in Adam's road tax.

Adam read it.

– Highway fee: Northern – One dollar seventy; Main road: 70 cents; Other: 14 cents. Why? – He looked at his wife.

– The eleventh! – said Nora angrily.

– So what? – Adam did not understand.

– On the eleventh you had an all-day meeting at your workplace. At least, that's what you told me. I remember because you were supposed to take Jake to the dentist. You even mentioned in the evening how tired you were from sitting all day long. So you didn't have any meetings that day. Where did you go up north? And why?

Adam stared at the letter.

– So? – Nora urged him.

– I had to do something there. – Adam shrugged his shoulders.

– Fester! – Do you hear that? He had something to do there. – Nora was indignant.

– I'm sorry, I cannot tell you my opinion in these types of arguments. My protocol prohibits it.

– Of course, now you don't intervene. You and your machine ethics! But you intervene when you have to tell me what to eat.

– That's one of my obligations.

– Obligation! – Nora continued. She turned back to Adam.

– So? What did you do there? – she asked him.

– It's not important.

– Yes, it is. Did you meet a woman?

– Oh my, just forget this stupid jealousy! I had something to do, let that be enough for now.

– But it's not enough! – Nora was getting angrier. – Where did you go?

– I'm not telling you. It's a secret.

– Don't play around with me, Adam! Answer me properly! We don't keep secrets from each other!

– Sure we do. – Adam shrugged his shoulders.

– But we cannot have secrets, – his wife fired back. – We are husband and wife. For good and for bad. We don't have secrets.

– Yes, we do.

– No, we can't.

– Yet, – Adam said, shrugging his shoulders again. – Everybody has secrets.

– I don't have any, – responded Nora, with pride.

– You do, – said Adam.

– No, I don't. And how would you know if I did have any, if they are secrets?

– If they are not kept properly, they come to light.

– OK, so tell me, what secret do you know?

– I don't want to put you in an awkward situation. – Adam turned back to looking at his mail.

– No! – said Nora. – You won't shake me off that easily.

– OK. – Adam leaned back and looked at his wife. – The white shoe box on the top shelf of the closet, among the winter pullovers. It's full of your love letters.

– Are you searching through my stuff? – Nora was flabbergasted.

– Nope. Didn't cross my mind. But if you keep your letters on the same shelf, in the same kind of box as the one I keep my revolver in, then sooner or later, I will accidentally take it down.

Nora blushed.

– Don't worry. I haven't read any of them. I saw what it was so I put it back.

– That's not a secret actually, – said Nora. – I just didn't talk about it.

– Good. You didn't tell me that your high-school sweetheart, David Gahan, found you on Facebook.

– He contacted me, – responded Nora, in confusion. – We had a little chat. A little nostalgia, nothing more. I haven't talked to him since.

– Sure. And the bouquet of roses in the garbage?

Nora's eyes flared up but Adam lifted his finger. – Before you say that I'm search your stuff even in the garbage, next time make sure that if you throw away the bouquet, throw something on it or don't send me out with the kitchen waste after that.

– It was from an acquaintance, – Nora said. – Since they didn't mean anything, I didn't even keep them.

– Then why did you keep it a secret?

– Because I didn't want it to be a problem. I didn't want you to feel bad because of it. And I didn't want a row, either.

Adam nodded. – To protect our relationship. Because sometimes we need secrets. They're necessary.

– All right. – Nora pulled herself up. – Now, it's your turn. What were you doing up north?

– It's a secret, – said Adam.

Suddenly, the doorbell rang.

– There are two unknown men at the door, – said Fester.

Nora stepped over to the door and opened it.

– Good evening, – Agent Noret greeted her politely. He showed his ID card. – Special agent Noret, FBI. This is my colleague, special agent Rose. Mrs. Nora East?

– Nora! The cards are authentic, – said Fester.

– Yes. Good evening. What can I do for you?

– We are looking for your husband, Mr. Adam East.

– He's at home.

– Can we talk to him?

– Adam! – Nora shouted into the kitchen. – Would you come here please? These people are looking for you.

Adam appeared at the door in a few moments. – Yes?

– Good evening. Special agent Noret and special agent Rose, FBI. Can we talk to you, sir?

Adam opened the door more widely with a surprised look and pointed inside the house.

– Come in, please.

– Thank you.

Adam took them into the living room and offered them a seat. Nora and Adam sat down opposite the agents.

– What is this about? Has there been a crime in the neighborhood?

– No, sir, it's about you.

– Me? – Adam sounded surprised.

– Yes. I would like to ask you a few questions so that we can finish as soon as possible.

– OK, go ahead.

– Have you purchased any fertilizer recently?

– Yes.

– In large quantities?

– Yes.

– When and how much?

– In the spring. I bought grass fertilizer in a five-kilo bucket and five kilos of general garden fertilizer.

Noret frowned. – Five kilograms?

– Yes.

– And since then? In the last month?

– Definitely not.

– I see. You are a sales manager, right?

– Yes.

– I assume you travel a lot.

Adam shrugged his shoulders. – As all sales managers do.

– When were you last in Kentucky?

– Not for a while.

– And in North Carolina?

– Same thing. These are not my regions.

– Virginia?

– Same thing. Well, actually yes.

– Yes?

– But it wasn't an official trip, rather a private trip.

– I see. – Noret reached into his pocket and took out something that looked like two thick pens. He pulled apart the two cylinders. An extra thin see-through foil was rolled out that quickly went hard. It switched on and the agent was holding a tablet in his hands. He tapped two icons and a document opened up. He handed it to Adam.

– Could you explain this to us?

– What's this? – Adam looked at the picture.

– There are several. Turn the pages.

Adam tapped the screen and new documents popped up. – I see, these are invoices. So what? – he asked.

– For the purchase of fertilizer.

– And? I still don't understand you.

– North Carolina: Kingsport, Greeneville, New Port. Kentucky: Manchester, Hazard, London. Ammonium nitrate was purchased at these places, several hundred kilograms each time.

– By whom?

– It seems it was you. The purchases were made with your data, your ID. Do you have a farm somewhere?

– What? Are you kidding me?

– Not at all. Look at the invoices.

Adam nervously flipped through them. – There must be a misunderstanding. I haven't bought any fertilizer. Not in that quantity.

Noret reached over the table and tapped on another icon. Additional invoices. – And what about the diesel oil? If I'm right, both of you have electric cars.

– Yes, I bought that.

– In Virginia?

– Yes?

– Can I ask you when and why?

– In the spring. Late spring. We went fishing with some friends and I rented a jeep. A four-wheel Jeep Wrangler. I filled it with fuel.

– Any other time?

– Nope.

– Adam, – said Nora. – There was another time.

– When? – asked Adam.

– The summer house.

– Oh, yeah – Adam lifted his head. – My father died at the end of the spring, I inherited a little wooden summer house from him in Virginia, near Roanoke, near the Washington national forest. We went there for a weekend, to pack things and to do some cleaning. The house has an oil boiler and I filled up its tank. I ordered around four hundred liters.

– Yes, that's right, – Nora agreed.

– Any other time? – inquired Rose.

– No, never.

Adam became anxious and asked Noret a little irritably.

– Agent Noret, would you tell us why you're here, please? And how long has the FBI been interested in the purchase of fertilizers and fuel?

Noret leaned back in the armchair. – We have been interested in it since AMFO, which is an explosive, was mixed for the first time from ammonium nitrate and diesel oil. Since terrorists started to use AMFO. Particularly, since 1995, when Timothy McVeigh blew up a government building in Oklahoma with AMFO.

Adam grew pale. – You have to be kidding me.

– No, sir, I'm not. At the FBI's counter terrorism unit we pay particular attention to this.

– Domestic terrorism? Are you accusing me of terrorism?

– Not yet, – Noret said. – Otherwise it wouldn't have been us who rang the door bell, a S.W.A.T. unit would have blown it up and now you would be sitting in an investigation room with a hood on your head.

– Jesus! – Nora's face went white.

Adam gulped. – I don't understand.

– One more question. Do you have a gun license?

– Yes.

– And what type of weapons do you have?

– I only have one. A Smith & Wesson M629 revolver. For self-defense.

– And are you expanding your stock of guns?

– I don't intend to.

– You haven't purchased any rifles?

– I told you, no.

– Well, Mr. East, the situation is as follows. One or more people purchased fertilizers, diesel oil and weapons in large quantities at a time in several states and cities. Separately the items are not too significant, but taken together they are. Particularly when only one name can be tied to these purchases: Adam East.

– It's impossible, – Adam said, stuttering. – It must be a misunderstanding. I haven't bought any fertilizers or weapons and I've only purchased diesel oil twice. My bankcards are OK. None of them have been lost. I have all of them.

– All the purchases were made with cash. This increased our suspicion. It is also suspicious that your wife made some strange transactions.

– Me? – said Nora, astounded.

– Yes. Ma'am. May I ask what kind of Islamic relations you have?

– Islamic relations? None. I like Arabic fashion, furniture, scarves, and jewels. I love Arabic cuisine, my favorite is Tunisian. We go to several Arabic restaurants or order dinner from them. I have a good relationship with one of the kebab sellers downtown. That's all.

– Foreign trips? Do you often travel to Arab countries?

– Not at all.

– We found something strange. According to your credit card records, you have been to many countries recently, and the point is, you made purchases in Algiers, Tunis, Tripoli, and Tangier. So you went to Libya, Tunisia, Algeria, and Morocco. In those places, terrorism is viewed differently than here.

However, according to the data of the airlines, Nora East has not flown to any such countries. We found only one trip: you went to Rome with your family.

– Oh, that's easy to explain, – Adam said. – My wife's purchases were made during the autumn, between 19 and 22 September, right?

Rose checked the list and nodded.

– I took my family for a little cruise on our wedding anniversary. But I didn't pay for a Caribbean cruise, it was in the Mediterranean. A round trip in the Western basin. From Rome to Rome. We woke up every morning in a different town. Rome-Palermo-Algiers-Tunis-Tripoli-Tangier-Gibraltar and so on. The stamps are there in our passports, along with the electronic signatures. I think you can also track it on the ship.

– This is great news, – said Noret. – It answers many of our questions. We will check this of course.

– And now, – said Rose. – Please give your consent for us to examine your phones and computers.

– No way, it's full of my personal stuff, – Nora said.

– Ma'am, I only requested for your approval as a matter of courtesy. Your cooperation is evidence of your good intent; on the other hand, although I didn't come with a S.W.A.T unit, I have a search warrant along with a phone search warrant and an IT search warrant.

– Then you will look at our photos and everything? – Nora asked.

– No, ma'am. The search will be done by a computer and it will only look for clues that hint at terrorism-related crimes. And we will essentially not do anything, let's say it's your phones that will testify about you.

– How? – Nora was surprised.

Rose spoke up. – According to federal law, all communication devices in the United States monitor their user's activity, and appropriately licensed authorities can query this data based on well-founded suspicions.

– What does this mean now? – Adam shook his head. – I don't understand.

– You phone has software that records and monitors what you use it for. If I have a phone search warrant in respect to a specific case, I can query the data specific to the given case from the phone. But only for this one case.

Noret displayed a new document. – Here it is. The authenticated phone search warrant. But it's better for both of us if you just simply give your consent.

Adam put the two phones onto the table. – Of course, go ahead, – he said. – I have no secrets.

– Thank you. It's just a press of a button. – Noret sent over the digital file.

– House search. Phone search warrant, – Fester said. – Authenticated. Adam, Nora, If you think that the digital house search is not lawful or you feel that your private sphere is being violated, I can notify the appropriate legal aid organization.

– Not necessary, it's all right. Thank you, – Adam said.

– The phone is going to check itself for data, events and activities that could be suspicious, related to terrorism. But only after this. And it will send a report that can be used for both the investigation and at the court. Like a digital witness.

– We will check the house's system as well.

– Okay, – Adam said.

– House search. Home computers, electronic devices, intelligent home system, – Fester said. – Authentic. After a quiet beep, a message showed up on Noret's tablet.

– What is Art-Hur 4.1? – he asked Adam.

– The security system used at my company. – responded Adam. – ARTifical HURdler breaks up data into random pieces, dismantles them, mixes them, and encrypts the pieces separately. So it locks the data into an "artificial quarantine." The software sends the data there and only the quarantine knows where the individual pieces are. Then, if the software requests the data, it puts the pieces together again and sends them back. It's like a cloud service, only in data size.

– Would you release the protection? This is necessary for a complete search.

– Of course. – Adam looked into the camera and put his finger on it. – Finger print and iris scanner.

– When did you go on this cruise, Mr. East? – Rose asked abruptly, as if with a new thought.

– Our flight departed on 15 September, in the morning, and we got back on the thirtieth.

Rose took the table from Adam and started to turn the page. – Look at this – he showed it to Noret.

– What is it? – Adam asked.

– I think you're in luck. There were purchases during the two weeks while you were abroad. Both fertilizers and weapons were purchased.

– So what does this mean?

– That it wasn't you who made the purchases.

A few seconds later the result of the electronic house search was displayed.

– I have good and not so bad news, – said Noret. – The report verifies you, it is more proof of your innocence.

– And what is the not so bad news? – asked Adam.

– You, Mr. East, have been a victim of identity theft. Someone obtained your personal data, IDs and who knows what else. Either the thieves are using it, or they sold it on the black market. Those who are using it are very likely terrorists.

– So what now?

– We will file our report, on the basis of which I'm sure that the investigation will be dropped against you. You were very lucky with this trip. Those who stole your data are professionals, they make sure that you do not detect the theft. That's why they pay in cash for example. I wouldn't be surprised if they received all the notifications and they just send them to you after filtering the information. At the last moment they'd definitely empty all of your accounts. Or something far worse could also happen. They would blackmail you or your kids, threatening to disclose your secrets. You would have to pay in exchange, or do something for them. This can have even more serious consequences. Or they would simply delete everything. I have seen several cases where victims got into trouble this way.

– What should we do now?

– I recommend that you replace your entire digital life. Change all of your passwords. Terminate all of your bank accounts and open new ones. Apply for new IDs, driving licenses, tax numbers, everything. Not only for you, but for the kids too. After the investigation we will issue a certificate of identity theft, so you will be able to receive the new documents.

– Man, that will take weeks.

– Probably, – said Noret. – After this, try to take better care of your secrets.

– Adam! – Fester said. – I have a protocol that indicates what should be done in cases like this. I can do some of it automatically myself if I receive the authorization, I will launch the process.

– I don't know, – Adam said. – Which is worse. The fact that they stole my life or that there is a ready-made protocol for such cases.

Noret looked at Rose. – We're done here. Let's go.

They shook hands at the door. – I would like to thank you, special agent, – said Adam.

– For what? – Noret sounded surprised.

– That you came yourself and didn't send the S.W.A.T team.

Noret waved, and he and Rose walked away.

Inside, Adam and Nora slumped onto the couch.

We were this close to spending our night at the police station, – said Adam. – Or worse.

– So what do we do now? – Nora asked.

– We'll take a holiday tomorrow. We'll go to the bank and everywhere else that he said.

– Adam!

– Yes?

– There's only one thing you didn't tell me.

– What?

– What were you doing up north?

– I'm fed up with this. – Adam stood up. He went out to the garage and came back with a large box. He threw it over to his wife and slumped back onto the couch.

– What's this?

– This is what you are interested in. The secret.

Nora opened the box. There was a beautiful hand-embroidered coat inside.

Adam started to speak: – I noticed last summer how much you liked these coats at the fair. I contacted the person who makes them and I had one made for your size, with your favorite colors.

I picked them up on the eleventh.

Nora went pale. Adam stood up and took the box away. – It was your Christmas surprise. But it won't be a surprise at Christmas anymore. This is how you will stand under the tree. Isn't it nice that we don't have secrets from each other?

NOTES

Used online resources

http://www.wsj.com/articles/rarely-patched-software-bugs-in-home-routers-cripple-security-1453136285

https://cups.cs.cmu.edu/soups/2014/workshops/privacy/s2p1.pdf

https://www.theguardian.com/technology/2010/jan/11/facebook-privacy

https://www.theguardian.com/uk/2004/dec/13/sciencenews.research

http://www.scientificamerican.com/article/why-do-we-forget-things/

https://www.linkedin.com/pulse/how-facebook-affects-our-privacy-behavior-walter-snell

https://www.theguardian.com/technology/2014/dec/14/sony-pictures-email-hack-greed-racism-sexism

http://www.advocate.com/hiv-aids/2015/11/17/watch-charlie-sheen-comes-out-hiv-positive

https://nakedsecurity.sophos.com/2016/04/28/suspect-who-wont-decrypt-hard-drives-jailed-indefinitely

https://www.eff.org/deeplinks/2012/03/tale-two-encryption-cases

http://news.softpedia.com/news/belgian-bank-loses-70-million-to-classic-ceo-fraud-social-engineering-trick-499388.shtml

http://news.softpedia.com/news/companies-lost-1-2-billion-1-07-billion-to-business-email-scams-490432.shtml

https://www.theguardian.com/technology/2016/may/10/court-refuses-request-force-alleged-hacker-lauri-love-hand-over-passwords

https://youtu.be/hzNQwqhotOs

http://tech.firstpost.com/news-analysis/al-jazeeras-mobile-news-service-hacked-39957.html

http://www.independent.co.uk/news/world/europe/tv5monde-hack-jihadist-cyber-attack-on-french-tv-station-could-have-russian-link-10311213.html

https://www.wired.com/2016/06/meet-ourmine-security-group-hacking-ceos-celebs/

http://9to5google.com/2014/07/02/goldman-sachs-taking-legal-action-against-google-to-retrieve-a-misaddressed-email/

http://www.wsj.com/articles/SB10001424127887324310104578511093691315014

http://www.mailermailer.com/resources/metrics/2016/bounce-rates.rwp

http://index.hu/kulfold/2016/07/20/5_millio_dan_szemelyes_adatait_kuldtek_el_kinanak_veletlenul/

http://resourcemagonline.com/2014/12/infographic-there-will-be-one-trillion-photos-taken-in-2015/45332/

https://ciip.wordpress.com/2009/06/21/a-list-of-reported-scada-incidents/

http://www.theregister.co.uk/2001/10/31/hacker_jailed_for_revenge_sewage/

http://krebsonsecurity.com/2016/07/the-value-of-a-hacked-company/

https://prezi.com/mhcwubuafqfi/norms-folkways-mores-taboos-and-laws/

http://www.nasdaq.com/article/infographic-data-breaches-grow-more-personal-cm587750

https://moly.hu/konyvek/hankiss-elemer-proletar-reneszansz

https://www.linkedin.com/pulse/why-hipaa-matters-medical-id-theft-human-cost-health-privacy-solove

http://www.bbc.com/news/magazine-26089486

https://www.reddit.com/r/ftm/comments/4dvjk6/guys_who_transitioned_postcollegedid_you_come_out/

http://www.forbes.com/pictures/mef45ggld/1-saudi-aramco-12-5-million-barrels-per-day/#6e0df1c713b0

http://www.bbc.com/news/business-36254238

http://money.cnn.com/2015/08/05/technology/aramco-hack/

https://www.sans.org/reading-room/whitepapers/analyst/security-spending-trends-36697

https://youtu.be/vRULr2kD6GE

http://tizenharomezredik.tumblr.com/post/55193775025/mit-tud-egy-v%C3%B6d%C3%B6r

http://gizmodo.com/is-this-vigilante-group-fighting-isis-or-just-feeding-t-1755489934

https://blog.osvdb.org/

http://www.nytimes.com/2016/06/09/technology/software-as-weaponry-in-a-computer-connected-world.html

http://www.huffingtonpost.ca/matthew-held/business-emails_b_5955124.html

http://www.nytimes.com/2015/02/08/style/15-minutes-of-fame-more-like-15-seconds-of-nanofame.html?_r=0

http://www.pewresearch.org/fact-tank/2015/05/29/what-americans-think-about-nsa-surveillance-national-security-and-privacy/

http://www.pewinternet.org/2015/05/20/americans-views-about-data-collection-and-security/#few-feel-they-have-a-lot-of-control-over-how-much-information-is-collected-about-them-in-daily-life

http://www.ncbi.nlm.nih.gov/pmc/articles/PMC4047123/

https://www.apa.org/news/press/releases/2015/08/reframing-sexting.pdf

http://www.ranum.com/security/computer_security/archives/internet-attacks.pdf

http://www.forbes.com/sites/thomasbrewster/2015/10/06/mystery-white-team-vigilante-hackers-speak-out/#18917b355a14

https://xakep.ru/2016/02/10/white-team-vs-lizard-squad/&prev=search

http://www.apple.com/customer-letter/

https://www.engadget.com/2016/01/14/nsa-us-freedom-act-transparency-report/

https://www.troyhunt.com/100-data-breaches-later-have-i-been-pwned-gets-its-first-self-submission/

https://www.troyhunt.com/when-nation-is-hacked-understanding/

https://www.wired.com/2016/02/encryption-is-worldwide-yet-another-reason-why-a-us-ban-makes-no-sense/

http://fortune.com/2016/07/10/wall-street-blockchain-technology-banking/

http://www.indiawest.com/news/global_indian/researchers-develop-app-that-can-hack-into-smart-home-security/article_06f02168-1609-11e6-ba5f-4f65a39c910d.html

http://www.extremetech.com/computing/133448-black-hat-hacker-gains-access-to-4-million-hotel-rooms-with-arduino-microcontroller

http://www.datasciencecentral.com/profiles/blogs/that-s-data-science-airbus-puts-10-000-sensors-in-every-single

https://youtu.be/001sbokYiJc (Paul's Security Weekly - Episode 417: Interview With Chris Roberts)

http://www.slate.com/articles/technology/future_tense/2016/05/the_aviation_industry_is_starting_to_grapple_with_cybersecurity.html

https://twitter.com/sidragon1

https://www.hackread.com/samsung-smart-tv-listening-conversations/

http://news.bbc.co.uk/2/hi/6057734.stm

https://youtu.be/--TfH82bTi8 (Dr. George Church — Brain healthspan extension)

https://youtu.be/GSVIKC4R2Zo (Prof. George Church - The Augmented Human Being)

https://youtu.be/giuVfY-I-p4 (Stephen Wolfram - AI & The Future Of Civilization)

http://www.cio.com/article/3019587/innovation/the-business-of-bots-and-the-realities-of-enterprise-automation.html

http://www.theatlantic.com/technology/archive/2015/12/peace-out-bots/419739/

https://points.datasociety.net/how-to-think-about-bots-1ccb6c396326#.rife4435e

http://www.bbc.com/news/uk-politics-19993921

https://www.theguardian.com/media/2007/oct/18/digitalmedia.advertising

http://fortune.com/2015/12/07/high-paying-cybersecurity-jobs-go-begging-across-the-world/

https://www.justsecurity.org/24823/half-life-secrets/

http://time.com/3858309/attention-spans-goldfish/

https://umdfire154.wordpress.com/projects-2016/

https://www.researchgate.net/publication/301279455_Communicating_crisis_uncertainty_A_review_of_the_knowledge_gaps

http://www.computerweekly.com/feature/Apollo-11-The-computers-that-put-man-on-the-moon

http://www.forbes.com/forbes/2001/0305/193.html

http://www.businessinsider.com/drone-pilots-say-their-job-is-not-like-playing-a-video-game-2012-9

http://www.gq.com/story/drone-uav-pilot-assassination

http://www.huffingtonpost.com/marilynne-k-roach/9-reasons-you-might-have-_b_4029745.html

http://www.keptelenseg.hu/viccek/monty-python-gyalog-galopp-25650

http://www.sacred-texts.com/neu/mphg/mphg.htm

http://www.southampton.ac.uk/news/2016/02/5d-data-storage-update.page

https://sg.hu/cikkek/117521/5d-s-adattarolast-fejlesztettek-brit-kutatok

https://news.samsung.com/global/samsung-mass-producing-industrys-first-512-gigabyte-nvme-ssd-in-a-single-bga-package-for-more-flexibility-in-computing-device-design

https://www.coloribus.com/adsarchive/tv-commercials/mobile-communications-equipment-retail-stores-sauna-424705/

http://www.nytimes.com/2016/05/06/technology/former-officer-is-jailed-months-without-charges-over-encrypted-drives.html

https://www.goodreads.com/quotes/283433-when-you-are-dealing-with-an-invisible-enemy-use-most

http://wais.stanford.edu/Democracy/democracy_DemocracyAndChurchill(090503).html

http://dailycaller.com/2016/08/12/bill-clinton-email-classification-issues-are-too-complicated-to-explain-to-people-video/

https://en.wikipedia.org/wiki/List_of_Latin_phrases_(R)#cite_note-2

https://www.youtube.com/watch?v=sOO_oYZF_B0

http://edition.cnn.com/2014/06/03/travel/737-emergency-pilot/

http://beszed.blog.hu/2015/07/10/kennedy_ugy_dontottunk_hogy_eljutunk_a_holdra

http://www.digitaltrends.com/cool-tech/japanese-ai-writes-novel-passes-first-round-nationanl-literary-prize/

https://www.ft.com/content/be26fbd2-5005-11e6-88c5-db83e98a590a

http://members.iif.hu/visontay/ponticulus/rovatok/humor/karinthy_tanar5.html

ARTHUR KELETI:
THE IMPERFECT SECRET

This book is about the smallest and most delicate asset that anyone and everyone possesses: our secrets. And I have bad news for you: our secrets are under threat, just when we thought they were in the most secure place that they could possibly be. Something happened, and it's irreversible, and still not fully understood. Don't think about those small secrets that are easy to share, or lose, or bring out into the light of day. Think about your most hidden, perhaps even forgotten secrets, things that could ruin your life, or the life of your loved ones; or bring down a company's reputation, damage its profits, or just tear the whole thing into pieces. Remember the VW emissions scandal? Just insert the name of your company! Pretty scary, no? And now for the good news. I partnered with a good friend and social-psychology expert, Zsuzsanna Szvetelszky, and took a good look at where the world is heading. Should we really share everything with each other? Can a secret-service exist any longer, where secrets will remain secrets? In the future, will we know everything about our politicians, company leaders, or the family living across the street? What is a secret anyhow? Why are they so important for us? Critical and complicated times are ahead, from the point of view of sociologists and information theorists, and we need to change the way we protect our data. In this book you'll find some practical advice and observations, to offer some answers for the emerging challenges of the new world that is already arriving.

www.ingramcontent.com/pod-product-compliance
Lightning Source LLC
Chambersburg PA
CBHW051225050326
40689CB00007B/810